Billy Watson's Croker Sack

Also by Franklin Burroughs

The River Home: A Return to the Carolina Low Country

Billy Watson's Croker Sack

ESSAYS BY Franklin Burroughs

The University of Georgia Press

Athens and London

Published in 1998 by the University of Georgia Press
Athens, Georgia 30602
© 1991 by Franklin Burroughs
All rights reserved
The paper in this book meets the guidelines for
permanence and durability of the Committee on
Production Guidelines for Book Longevity of the
Council on Library Resources.
Printed in the United States of America
02 01 00 99 98   P   5 4 3 2 1

Library of Congress Cataloging in Publication Data
Burroughs, Franklin.
Billy Watson's croker sack / Franklin Burroughs.
p.   cm.
Originally published: New York : W.W. Norton, c1991.
ISBN 0-8203-1999-6 (pbk. : alk. paper)
1. Hunting. 2. Fishing.   I. Title.
[SK33.B94   1998]
799—dc21   97-34307

British Library Cataloging in Publication Data available
Previously published in paper by Houghton Mifflin Company in 1992

"A Snapping Turtle in June," "Of Moose and a Moose Hunter,"
and "Dawn's Early Light" all appeared originally in the *Georgia Review;*
"A Pastoral Occasion" was first published in the *Kenyon Review.*

The engraving of a snapping turtle is by Thomas Cornell,
of Bowdoin College, and is used here by permission.

To the several generations:
GBB and FGB; SHB;
Coco, Liz, and Hannah.

My first thanks go to Deanne Urmy, whose practical sagacity, literary judgment, generosity, and candor helped greatly in the initiating and sustaining of the whole enterprise.

Stanley Lindberg, of *The Georgia Review*, has been encouraging and acute.

Contents

Contents

Billy Watson's Croker Sack

1 🐢 A Snapping Turtle in June

All that can usefully be said about New England weather has been said. It is arbitrary, precipitate, and emphatic, less certain than a baby's bottom. Like the mind, it isn't necessarily bound by chronology. April can suddenly hearken back to February; a few hours in January will be as balmy as a May afternoon—that is, as one of those rare May afternoons that aren't recollecting March or daydreaming about September. Here on an overcast Tuesday morning late in June, it is summer sure enough, yet we must depend more upon the floral calendar than the thermometer for corroboration. We've had one spell of hot weather—temperature into the 90's, high humidity, bread going moldy in a day, crackers limp as old lettuce—but that was two weeks ago, and it has been cool since then, either rainy and chill or bright and breezy and autumnal.

But the flowers keep their seasons. Our fields, especially the poorer one that lies between the house and the river, are rich in

3

buttercup and vetch, lesser stitchwort, fragrant bedstraw, and blue-eyed grass. From the standpoint of agriculture, these plants are weeds, and therefore absolutely reliable. Cold, wet, and drought do not deter them; the only way to thwart them is by herbicide or fertilizer. The buttercups are long-stemmed and grow in all but the lushest pastures. Vetch, called partridge-pea in South Carolina, grows in little tangles of vine, like untrellised morning glories, as do stitchwort and bedstraw, and so they fare best in a thin, ledgy, or sandy soil, where the grass is meager. On a moist, unsummery summer morning, these flowers make soft clots and smears of color throughout the watery green of the pasture grasses. Thriving amid the adversities of soil and climate, their inconspicuous beauty seems reflective of rural New England, and it is pleasing to learn that people here once found more than aesthetic solace in them. Stitchwort was so named because it was thought to cure "stitches"—pains in the side, of the sort that runners get—while bedstraw was used to lie upon, back when a bed was a board, covered with straw, covered with a sheet. Fragrant bedstraw is quite odorless in life, but reputedly grows savory in death, when sufficiently dried.

Except for the vetch, we had nothing in South Carolina like these field flowers or the daisies and hawkweed that populate the road shoulders at this season of the year, and there is not a great deal in the Maine summer that particularly recalls the summers of my Southern boyhood. But that strange Wordsworthian hunger for landscape, growing out of an individual and cultural maturity, is complexly regressive, and involves much attempted calling back of things that probably exist only in the echo of the caller's voice. Fewer and fewer of us have Wordsworth's privilege of inhabiting as adults the landscape we inhabited as children, and of learning to recognize in it what he called "the language of my former heart." Even if luck and resolution enable us eventually to live in places of great beauty and interest, there is some quality of internal exile that shadows our relation to them.

A Snapping Turtle in June

This is a particular problem if you are a non–New Englander who comes to live in New England. New England is an image ready-made for you, no matter where you come from. It has so defined the American conception of landscape, and of the ideal human response to landscape, that it is not easy to arrive at a direct relation to it. It's rather like being married to a celebrity—your own response responds to a simplified and magnified public perception, as well as to the thing itself. Or, as a friend of mine, a tough-minded New Yorker, observed to me one November day, while we sat in a skiff in Broad Cove, looking across blue water that glinted and sparkled as though it were already full of ice shards, through crystal air and toward the shore with its patchwork of fields, woodlots, and bleak, bone-white houses gleaming in the sun: "Who are they trying to kid? This is the most *derivative* goddamned landscape I've ever seen in my life."

Boyhood was once almost as distinct a part of the American terrain as New England is, and, like New England, it had its heyday in the nineteenth century, and continued to be valued because, until fairly recently, it went on evoking the life of that century. There is the image of a sandy or a dusty road, the feel of the road under the feet, the cane pole carried over the shoulder, the drone of cicadas, the hair warm from the sun: the barefoot boy with cheeks of tan, the etchings and engravings of Winslow Homer, and supremely and inevitably, *Tom Sawyer* and *Huckleberry Finn*. In contrast, *girlhood* does not seem to generate this mirage. It doesn't evoke the same semitribal life, the living in a world rather closer to the wordless world of smells, itches, and yapping contentions of the unregulated dogs of small-town America than to the world of adults, or even to the world of the sort of regimented, housebroken, neurotic, pedigreed canines that one finds in the houses of one's friends.

There is of course much compensatory distortion in this image of boyhood, but I do not think it is altogether false. The boredom was as thick as the heat in Conway, South Carolina, and one

5

learned to relish both in the summers. In our neighborhood, which is now an attractive suburban network of streets overhung with water oaks and sycamores, the streets were not yet paved—there was still a lot of unpaved road in the South at that time—and that gave, in a small way, texture and variety to life. In rainy seasons, the roads were slick and the puddles would turn to bogs, rutted out and mucky; occasionally a car, ineptly driven by one of the ladies of the neighborhood, would get stuck. But by summer the sun would have baked the roads hard beneath the dust that powdered them, and boys wore shoes only under compulsion. That is not possible where the streets are asphalt, and the tar sticks to your feet like napalm. I think girls wore shoes more regularly, in the fashion of their sisters in cities, but many of my impressions of girlhood must have been taken from my own sister, who was four years older and that much more aware of the world beyond the doorstep. In any event, I tended to associate femininity with paved streets, and knew for a fact that it was the ladies of the neighborhood, my own mother not excepted, who were most insistent that the roads be paved, so that they would not get stuck in the rainy weather, or have their children tracking mud into the house or getting their feet full of ringworm. From listening to them, you would have thought that they were the Victorian wives of British colonials, suddenly finding themselves in the Burmese or Australian outback, amid conditions of an appalling primitiveness.

At that time, the paved road stopped at the railroad tracks, about a quarter mile from our house. Then one day my great friend Ricky McIver and I walked down to the railroad tracks, preparing to follow them, as we were forbidden to do, along the causeway that ran through the swamps and eventually reached the trestle over Kingston Lake. But there, where the pavement ended, was a roadblock and a detour sign, apologizing for the inconvenience and announcing that this section of the road was to be surfaced. It was the beginning of a lifetime of symbolic Luddite resistance. We pushed over the roadblock, which was no more than a sawhorse, and threw the sign into the ditch beside the road. To no avail, needless to say: the road got paved anyway. History does not leave the backwaters of boyhood alone, and Ricky would soon enough find himself personifying it to barefoot villagers, who liked it no better than he had, in dusty hamlets, full of yapping dogs, outside Da Nang.

We were not, of course, thinking of pavement in terms of abstractions like History or Progress. It might have crossed our minds that its coming would mean that we had to wear shoes, or that more dogs would be run over, because cars would travel so much faster on the asphalt, and the dogs, like the children, thought of the streets as places of concourse and recreation. But probably nothing even that theoretical occurred to us. I think it was that we were mostly considering the snapping turtles that would, some time in the middle of every summer, appear in the road—sturdy little fellows, their shells not much bigger than a silver dollar. Paving the road would be the end of them.

All these things came to mind on this Tuesday morning in Maine, with the fields full of flowers and late June imitating early May, because, as I started out down the gravel road that connects our house to the highway, and drew abreast of the little quarter-acre pond that sits to the left of the road, here was, large as life and squarely in my way, a big mama snapping turtle, excavating herself a hole to lay her eggs in. I was in no particular hurry, and so I stopped and got out to investigate. Snappers are the most widely distributed of North American turtles, and they are by no means uncommon in Maine, but they are normally reclusive, and when one makes a public appearance it is not an event to be passed over lightly. This particular one certainly had no intention of being passed over lightly: if she had intended to blockade the road, she couldn't have chosen a better spot.

Several things distinguish them from other freshwater turtles, most obviously their size. The one at my feet was about two feet long, from the tip of her snout to the tip of her tail. When I

eventually picked her up by the tail (and that is another distin-
guishing feature of snapping turtles—you pick up an ordinary turtle by the rim of its shell, but a snapper's neck is remarkably long
and flexible, so you grab the creature by the tail and hold it well
out from your body), I guessed she weighed a good twenty pounds.

The general proportions of a snapping turtle are wrong. The
head is far too big; the shell is too little. The plastron, or under-
shell, is ridiculously skimpy—it seems barely adequate for the
purposes of decency, and as useless as a bikini would be as far as
anatomical protection is concerned. Consequently a snapper cannot withdraw into itself as other turtles do. It retracts the head
enough to shield its neck and doesn't even attempt to pull in its
legs and feet. The legs and tail are large in relation to the body:
when a snapper decides to walk it really *walks;* the bottom of the
shell is a couple of inches off the ground, and, with its dorsally
tuberculate tail, long claws, and wickedly hooked beak, it looks
like a scaled-down stegosaur.

A Snapping Turtle in June

A snapper compensates for its inadequate armor in a variety of ways, the most immediately apparent of which is athletic ability combined with a very bad temper. It can whirl and lunge ferociously, and, if turned over on its back, can, with a thrust and twist of its mighty neck, be upright and ready for mayhem. If you approach one out of water, it opens its mouth and hisses; if you get closer, it lurches at you with such vehemence that it lifts itself off the ground, its jaws snapping savagely at empty air. Archie Carr, whose venerable *Handbook to Turtles* (1952) is the only authority on these matters I possess, states that the disposition to strike is innate, and has been observed in hatchlings "not yet altogether free of their eggshells." An adult can strike, he reports, "with the speed and power of a big rattlesnake." Although Carr does not explicitly say so, the snapper appears to be one of those animals, like the hognose snake, that makes the most of its resemblance to a poisonous snake. Its pale mouth gapes open like a moccasin's, and its aggressiveness involves a certain exaggerated and theatrical posturing. Its official name specifically and subspecifically suggests the highly unturtlelike impression that this creates: *Chelydra serpentina serpentina.* But the snapper, unlike the hognose, can back up its bluff. Its first-strike capability isn't lethal, but it isn't trivial either. According to boyhood folklore, a snapper can bite a broomstick in two, but I have seen the experiment conducted. It took a great deal of goading to persuade the turtle to seize the broomstick at all—it plainly would have preferred the hand that held it—but it finally took it, held it, and crushed and pulped it. Mama's broom handle came out looking like a piece of chewed-over sugarcane. Putting your hand in range of a big snapper would not be like putting it under a guillotine or axe; it would be more like putting it under a bulldozer: a slow, complete crunching.

The shell and skin are a muddy gray; the eye, too, is of a murky mud color. The pupil is black and shaped like a star or a spoked wheel. Within the eye there is a strange yellowish glint, as though you were looking down into turbid water and seeing, in the depths of the water, light from a smoldering fire. It is one of Nature's more nightmarish eyes. The eyes of dragonflies are also nightmarish, but in a different way—they look inhuman, like something out of science fiction. The same is true of the eyes of sharks. The snapper's eye is dull, like a pig's, but inside it there is this savage malevolence, something suggesting not only an evil intention toward the world, but the torment of an inner affliction. Had Milton seen one, he would have associated it with the baleful eye of Satan, an eye reflecting some internal hell of liquid fire, even in Paradise or here on a soft June day, with the bobolinks fluttering aloft and singing in the fields. Snapping turtles did in fact once inhabit Europe, but they died out by the end of the Pleistocene, and so were unknown to what we think of as European history. But they look, nevertheless, like something that Europeans had half-imagined or dimly remembered even before they came to the New World and saw them for the first time: a snapper would do for a gargoyle, or a grotesque parody of a knight on his horse, a thing of armored evil.

Snappers feed on about anything, dead or alive: fish, flesh, or fowl. The fish they catch by luring them into range with their vermiform tongues, which may have something to do with the role of trickster that they assume in the mythology of North American Indians. But they can also be caught in a trap baited with bananas. They are not fastidious: "Schmidt and Inger (1957) tell the gruesome story of an elderly man who used a tethered snapping turtle to recover the bodies of people who had drowned."* We do not learn what this sinister gentleman fed his useful pet to encourage its predilection for waterlogged cadavers. I know on my own authority that snappers are death on ducks, and will rise like a shadow from the oozy muck of the bottom, under the jocund and unsuspecting drake as it briskly preens and putters on the surface of the pond, lock sudden jaws around one suspended leg,

*Turtles: Perspectives and Research, ed. M. Harless and H. Morlock (New York: Wiley, 1979), p. 289.

one webbed foot, and sink quietly back to the depths, their weight too much for the duck to resist, their jaws a functional illustration of necessity's sharp pinch. There in the darkness the duck is ponderously mauled, mutilated, and eaten, right down to the toenails. We watched a hen mallard and a brood of ducklings disappear from the little pond beside the road one summer—two or three inexplicable deductions per week—until at last only the very nervous hen and one trusting little duckling remained. Then there was only the duckling. It peeped and chirped and swam distractedly around the pond in a most heart-rending fashion. I tried to trap it so we could rear it in confinement and safety, but there was no catching it, and the next day it was gone too.

The law of tooth and nail is all right with me when it involves hawks and mice, or foxes and geese, or even sharks and swimmers—there is a redeeming elegance in most predators, a breathtaking speed and agility. If I thought I could tempt an eagle to stoop, I'd gladly stake my best laying hen in the yard to see it happen. But a snapper is an ugly proposition, more like cancer than a crab is. If one grabs your finger, you do not get the finger back—that too is boyhood folklore, but I have never tested it. Some propositions call for implicit faith, even in these post-theological and deconstructing days.

Unlike most of the other freshwater turtles, snappers never emerge to bask on rocks or logs. They come out in late spring or early summer; their emergence here coincides with the vetch, the stitchwort, bedstraw, and hawkweed. They need sandy soil to lay their eggs in, and such soil isn't always close to the sorts of boggy, miry waters they inhabit. They will often go overland a surprising distance. Even so, Carr says that females will sometimes cross large areas of suitable terrain before finally deciding on a spot to dig. He waxes jocosely socio-biological: "This characteristic . . . may be seen in most nesting turtles and may indeed be homologous to the traditional urge in the human female to move the furniture about."

Billy Watson's Croker Sack

❧

Roadbeds and railway embankments can provide good sites that are reasonably convenient to their usual habitats. Creatures of darkness, cursing the light, they lumber up from pond or river, and one morning you awake to the frantic yapping of dogs and go out, and there, foul and hissing, like some chieftain of the underworld at last summoned to justice and surrounded by reporters and cameras, stands a great gravid snapper. The flesh of her neck, legs, and tail—all the parts that ought to fit inside the shell but don't—has, on the underside, a grimy yellowish cast to it, is podgy, lewd, wrinkled, and soft. In Maine there will normally be one or two big leeches hanging onto the nether parts. These portions of the animal seem to have no proper covering—no scales, feathers, hair, or taut, smooth epidermis. It looks as though the internal anatomy had been extruded, or the whole animal plucked or flayed.

I'm not sure how much of this natural history Ricky McIver and I understood when we were nine or ten; we only knew that, trekking down a sandy road in midsummer, we would suddenly come upon a baby snapper, bustling along with remarkable purpose, as though on its way to catch a train. Of course we would catch the turtle, and one of us would take it home and put it in a dishpan with some water and keep it under the bed, where all night long there would be the tinny scraping of little claws, as the turtle went round and round inside the pan. Sometimes one would escape, instigating a general panicky search of the room and the house. It would turn up far back under a sofa or cabinet, covered with dust and weakened by dehydration, but still able to muster a parched snap and hiss. Finally we would let it go into a drainage ditch. We never came upon a mother laying her eggs—given the heat, perhaps they did that at night down south. Up here I seem to come across one or two of them every year, and have learned to look for them along road shoulders in late June.

I backed the car up to the house to get Susan and Hannah—the older girls were still asleep—and our old pointer Jacob roused himself and walked down with us, conferring by his stiff-jointed, wheezing Nestorian solemnity an air of officialdom upon the occasion, as though we were a commission sent out to investigate an unregistered alien that had showed up in Bowdoinham. Hannah went along grudgingly, with a five-year-old's saving sense that any time the parents promised to show you something interesting, they probably had concealed motives of one sort or another. When we got to the turtle, Jacob hoisted his hackles, clapped his tail between his legs, and circled her a few times, then sat down and barked once. The turtle raised herself on her forelegs, head up, mouth agape; her hostility did not focus on any one of us so much as on the whole situation in which she found herself. Hannah looked at all of this and pronounced it boring; could she have a friend over to play? The dog seemed to feel that he had discharged his obligations by barking, and shambled over to the edge of the field, pawed fretfully at the ground, then settled himself, curled up, sighed, and went to sleep. The whole thing was beginning to take on the unpromising aspect of Nature Study, an ersatz experience.

We walked around behind the turtle, and there did make a discovery of sorts. Through all of the commotion that surrounded her anterior end, her hind legs were methodically digging. Their motion was impressively regular and mechanical—first one leg thrust down into the hole, then the other, smooth and steady as pistons. Whatever the snapper felt or thought about her situation plainly did not concern the legs, which were wholly intent on procreation. It seemed an awkward way to dig, the hind foot being a clumsy and inflexible instrument anyway, and having to carry on its operations huggermugger like that, out of sight and out of mind too, if the turtle could be said to have a mind. We could not see down into the hole, only the legs alternately reaching down, and a rim of excavated sand that was slowly growing up behind the rim of the turtle's shell. I was later to learn that the digging action, once begun, is as involuntary as the contractions of a mammal giving birth, and even a turtle missing one hind leg will dig in the same fashion, thrusting down first with the good leg, then with the amputated stump, until the job is done.

Hannah, an aficionado of the sandbox, permitted herself a cautious interest in this end of the turtle's operations, and wanted to inspect her hole. I wasn't sure about the ethics of this. It is a general law that you don't disturb nesting creatures; it was, after all, no fault of the snapper's if she failed to excite in us the veneration that generally attaches to scenes of maternity and nativity. On the other hand, she had chosen a bad place. I could see where my neighbor Gene Hamrick had carefully driven around her, going well over onto the shoulder to do so. Other neighbors might be less considerate, and the nest itself would, in any event, be packed hard by the traffic in a few weeks, rendering the future of the eggs and hatchlings highly uncertain. So I grasped her tail and hoisted her up. Aloft, she held herself rigidly spread-eagle, her head and neck parallel to the earth, and hissed mightily as I took her over and put her in the little ditch that drains the pond. Because of the recent rain, the ditch was flowing, and as soon as her front feet touched the water, all of her aggression ceased, and she seemed bent on nothing but escape. She had surprising power as she scrabbled at the banks and bottom of the ditch; it was like holding onto a miniature bulldozer. I let her go and she surged off down the ditch, head submerged and carapace just awash. She stopped once and raised her head and fixed us with her evil eye; the mouth dropped open in a last defiance. Then she lowered her head again and waddled out of sight.

We examined the hole. It looked as though it had been dug with a tablespoon—shapely and neat, a little wider at the bottom than at the top. There were no eggs. Hannah set methodically about refilling the hole, out of an instinct that seemed as compelling as the one that dug it. As she disturbed the sand, I caught a strong musky scent where the turtle had lain. That scent, which was also on my hand, recalled something that the sight of the turtle had not recalled, and that was a peculiar memory connected to the biggest snapping turtle I ever saw, or ever intend to see.

A Snapping Turtle in June

In my high school summers, I worked for the Burroughs Timber Company, which was owned by a group of my father's first cousins. My immediate boss was Mr. Henry Richards; the crew consisted of the two of us and two cousins, Billy and Wendell Watson. Mr. Richards was not an educated man, and had in his younger days been something of a drinker and a fighter, but he had straightened himself out and gotten some training in forestry. He was good at his job, as far as I could judge—his job largely consisting of cruising and marking timber, overseeing logging operations, and generally keeping track of the company's woodlands. These were mostly small tracts, seldom more than a few hundred acres, scattered from one end of Horry County to the other. Mr. Richards was handsome: lean and weathered, with dark wavy hair, sleepy eyes, and the sort of indolent rasping voice that conveyed the authority of someone who had not always been perfectly nice. He was in his forties. Billy and Wendell were younger by ten or fifteen years, and both were countrymen, from the vicinity of Crabtree Creek.

I am not sure what degree of cousinage joined Billy and Wendell. The Watsons, like the Burroughses and a great many other families in the county, were an extended and numerous clan, and such clans generally divided into what religion had taught us to regard as the children of promise and the children of perdition, or sheep and goats. The binary opposition would express itself in terms of whatever general station in life the family occupied. Thus my Burroughs cousins tended to be either sober, quietly respectable merchants and landowners concerned with tobacco and timber, or drunkards, wastrels, and womanizers, men notorious in Horry County for the frequency with which they married and divorced.

Wendell belonged to the reputable branch of the Watson family—small farmers who held onto their land and led hard, frugal lives. In town, such people were referred to, somewhat inscrutably, as the salt of the earth. Billy came from the other side—poachers, moonshiners, people likely to be handy with a straight

15

razor, who kept six or eight gaunt and vicious hounds, half of them stolen and all of them wormy, chained in the yard, along with a few unfettered chickens and a ragged mule, but who could hardly be called farmers. Their style of life and economy had probably been formed by the county's long history as a demifrontier, and had changed only minimally to accommodate the twentieth century when it eventually arrived.

Wendell was one of those rare country people who, out of some reaction to the dirt and despair of agriculture, had a highly developed fastidiousness. His face was bony, angular, and prim around the mouth; he always wore a dapper straw hat instead of the usual cap, so that his brow was never browned or reddened by the sun. His work shirt and pants were neatly creased, and I never saw them stained with sweat. He would stop for a moment in the resinous, stifling heat of a pine wood, extract a red bandanna handkerchief from his pocket, unfold it, and delicately dab at his brow, removing his hat to do so. Then he would look at the moist handkerchief the way you might look at a small cut or blister, with a slight consternation and distaste, and then fold the handkerchief, first into halves, then into quarters, then into eighths, until it fit back into his hip pocket as neatly as a billfold.

He was lanky, with comically large feet and big, bony, lightly freckled hands and wrists, and you would have expected him to have no strength or stamina at all. But he could use any of the tools we used—bushaxe or machete or grubbing hoe—with no sign of strain or fatigue, all day long, holding the tool gingerly, so that you expected him to drop it at any moment, but keeping a pace that the rest of us could not sustain. He had a crooked, embarrassed grin and said little. In the midday heat, sometimes we would take our lunch to an abandoned tenant house, to eat on the porch and catch whatever breeze funneled through the doorway. Then three of us would stretch out on the warped floorboards, hats over our faces, and doze for half an hour. Wendell never did. He would sit with his back to one of the rough timbers that held up the porch, pull out his pocket knife, and set about pruning his fingernails; then he would stick the knife into a floorboard with an air of finality, lift his head and stare out over the fields with the intense, noncommittal scrutiny of a poker player examining his cards, or of what he was, a countryman watching the big banks of cumulus clouds pile up on a July afternoon. Or he might whittle himself a toothpick and ply it carefully between his teeth, or study a map of the tract we were to cruise in the afternoon. He always kept a watch over himself, as though he feared he might otherwise grow slack and slovenly. He did not own a car, and was permitted to use the company truck to go to and from his house, and to keep it over the weekend. On Monday mornings it would be all washed and cleaned; Mr. Richards would ask him whether he'd been courting in it or was he just planning to sell it. Wendell would only laugh awkwardly at himself, and at his inability to think of a smart retort.

Billy Watson, to hear him tell it, was chiefly proud of having spent six years in the fourth grade, at the end of which time he was sixteen and not legally obligated to go to school anymore. Mr. Richards could not get over it. "Damn, Billy," he said more than once, "don't seem like you're *that* stupid." He'd say it because he relished Billy's invariable answer, always delivered in the same tone of pious resignation, as though he were speaking of some cross that the Lord had, in His ungovernable wisdom, given him to bear: "Oh, I wa'nt stupid. Just ornery." He was a big man, about six foot three, with powerful, rounded shoulders. He had a peculiar sort of physical complacence with himself, was loose and supple as a cat, and could squat or hunker longer and more comfortably, it seemed, than the average man could sit in an armchair. His hair was lank and reddish brown, and was usually seconded by a four- or five-day growth of stubble beard, stained with tobacco juice at the lower right corner of the mouth. It was a big, misshapen mouth, distended by the pouch in one cheek that is the outcome of a lifetime of chewing tobacco—Day's Work or Sun

Apple. His teeth were few and far between, worn and yellowed as an old mule's. He had certainly never been to a dentist in his life, and might have been surprised to learn that such a profession existed.

Billy was a river rat; if he could have, he would have lived by doing nothing but trapping and fishing. He sometimes fished for sport: he could handle his stubby casting rod as though he had a kind of intelligence in his hands, placing each cast, cast after cast, far back under overhanging trees, with no pause, no hesitation, no calculation of the risks of getting the plug hung on a branch or snag. There was so much rhythm in it that you'd find yourself patting your foot if you watched him long enough. But he wasn't particular about how he caught fish or what fish he caught: redbreast, bream, goggle-eye, stumpknocker, warmouth, bass, catfish, eel, mudfish, redfin pike, shad, Virginia perch—even the herring that ran upriver in the spring.

If early on a Saturday morning in the spring you happened to be down by Mishoe's Fish Market, a little frame building perched by the edge of Kingston Lake, you might see Billy slipping easily along the near bank of the lake, in a ridiculously undersized one-man paddling boat. He'd give you a look before he drew up to the landing, ask you if there was anybody there. You'd look around for only one thing, a yellow car with a long antenna, because that might be someone from the state fish and game department, which kept an eye on Mr. Mishoe. Not seeing it, you'd say no, nobody here but old man Mishoe. There was a strange, watery peace to it. All the drab, ordinary life of the town was just a few hundred feet away, but here was Billy gliding silently up to the landing, dropping the paddle with muffled reverberation into the boat bottom, then stepping out, shackling the little boat to a cypress, and bending over to lift from it two moist croker sacks, each squirming with his night's work. You'd want to follow him through the fish market to the back, where Mr. Mishoe and one or two helpers would be cleaning and filleting fish. They'd stop to watch Billy empty his sacks into a cleaning sink—the secret, active ingredients of river and river swamp, wriggling, flapping, and gasping there in the back room of a store. The catfish, mudfish, eels, and shad were classified as nongame species and could, within certain limits, be fished and marketed commercially. The rest were pure contraband, which presumably increased their market value. Whatever that value was, Billy would receive it in a few greasy bills, walk up to the drugstore on Main Street, and buy himself a cup of coffee and a doughnut. Townspeople who did not know him would edge away from the counter: he was a dirty, rough-looking man, unlaced boots flapping open at his ankles. His eyes, which were small and deep-set, reflected light strangely; they were green, and, in the strict sense of the word, *crazed*, as though the surface of the eye were webbed with minute cracks. You could not tell where they focused.

But Billy wasn't crazy or violent either, as far as I ever heard. Education is liberating in ways it does not always intend, and, by keeping Billy in the fourth grade, surrounded, year after year, by an unaging cohort of ten-year-olds, it liberated him from most notions of responsibility, foresight, or ambition. He had successfully learned how to avoid promotion, a lesson that ought to be learned and taught more often than it is. He had worked out at the plywood mill, upriver from Conway, and told me he had also done some house painting. But working for Mr. Richards and Burroughs Timber suited him best, and he was a valuable employee. He probably knew more about the company land than the company did, having hunted, fished, or trapped on most of it. When we would cruise timber, one of us would set the compass course for him, and then he could follow it, keeping careful count of his paces, marking each of the stations where we would stop and inventory all the timber in a quarter-acre plot, while Billy went ahead to the next station and marked the next plot. Often we would end the day on the back line of a tract, a long way from the truck. The logical thing in thick woods was to plot a course back to the truck and follow the compass out, but Billy would drop the compass into his pocket and strike off through the woods as nonchalantly as a man going across a parking lot. We'd follow. He did everything in such a headlong, unconsidering way that those of us who had gotten beyond the fourth grade could never bring ourselves to trust him entirely, and sooner or later somebody would call out: "Billy, you *sure* this is the right way?" "Time'll tell, boys; time'll tell," he'd call back. Time always did, and we would suddenly emerge from the woods, and there would be the road, and there would be the truck. Townspeople who knew Billy lost no occasion to point him out to you: "That's Billy Watson. Ain't got a lick of sense, but you won't find a better fisherman in this county."

We were working down toward the Pee Dee River, on a low, sandy ridge at the edge of the river swamp. The company had cleared the ridge two or three years earlier and planted it in pine seedlings, but now the hardwoods, regenerating from the stump, threatened to reclaim it for themselves. The smaller hardwoods we chopped down with machete or bushaxe; the larger ones we girdled—gouged a ring around the trunk, half an inch deep, which cut off the tree's supply of food and water, and left it to die on its feet. For this we had a machine called the Little Beaver. It consisted of a four-cycle Briggs and Stratton engine mounted on a packframe, with a flexible hydraulic hose, at the end of which was a notched disk that did the girdling. The machine seemed to have no muffler at all—it was louder than a chainsaw, hot on the back, and the noise and vibration of it were stunning. It was late July, and that sandy patch of scrub oak and seedling pine afforded no protection from the sun. We would trade off the Little Beaver at thirty-minute intervals; not even Wendell volunteered to take any more of its hammering than that.

At noon, as was the custom, we knocked off. Mr. Richards

drove out to the Georgetown highway. He knew of a country store across the river, over in Georgetown County, and proposed to take us there for lunch. It was owned by a man named Marlowe. I'd seen it often enough, the usual little mean, flat-topped cinder-block building, painted white, with a screened door for ventilation, within which you could expect to find the standard items: canned goods, bread, a bit of fishing tackle, and one or two coolers full of soft drinks and milk. As we drove, Mr. Richards talked about the Marlowes, and we learned that they were an infamous clan, divided into two subspecific groups which intermingled freely: the regular Marlowes and the murdering Marlowes. If you insulted a regular Marlowe—for example, by catching him stealing your boat—he would, within a week or ten days, set your woodlot on fire, slash your tires, or shoot your dog. But if you did the same thing to a murdering Marlowe, why then your troubles were over—instantly and permanently. That is what Mr. Richards said, but he was something of a talker and not above hyperbole. We didn't take it seriously and probably weren't meant to. Wendell didn't say much—he never did—but he had a tight little grin and plainly didn't believe what he was hearing. Billy was keeping his eye on the swamp and river as we crossed over them—the Pee Dee was outside his usual territory, and he'd been talking all morning about how he aimed to fish her this fall, from Gallivant's Ferry clear down to Yauhannah Bridge, where we were now. When we pulled off the highway and parked in the thin shade of an oak beside Marlowe's store, Mr. Richards said for us to remember to act polite; we didn't need any trouble with these folks, and neither did Burroughs Timber.

When you walk out of the dazzle of noon into a little roadside store like that, it is almost like walking into a movie theater, the darkness seems so great. By the door was a counter with a cash register on it and a man behind it, and there was a shadowy figure in the back of the store, who turned out to be a boy younger than myself, sweeping the single aisle between the shelves. And there was a figure seated to the left of the door as I came in, and on the floor, at my feet, there was a sudden lunging rush.

If you have gotten this far, you have the advantage of knowing that it was, of course, a snapping turtle, but I did not. In the South Carolina woods in the summertime, snakes are never far out of your mind, and, for the first hour of the day, you watch your step. Fatigue and distraction set in soon enough, and you forget about snakes, and you could easily go two weeks without having any particular reason to remember them. But sooner or later you would come upon one, usually a little copperhead, neatly coiled at your feet, and so perfectly merged with the shadow-dappled floor of the forest that you'd begin to worry about all the ones that you hadn't happened to see. So when I heard the hiss and the rush I jumped.

The man in the chair laughed: "Scared you, didden he? I be goddam if you didden *jump*, boy. Don't believe I ever knew a white boy to jump like that." By this time I could see what it was, a snapping turtle stretched out there on the cement floor. It was a huge one—the carapace was matted with dried algae; the head was about the size of a grapefruit. The whole creature could not have been fitted into a washtub. It looked, once I had calmed down enough to look at it, ancient and tired, as though oppressed by its own ponderous and ungainly bulk. The room was thick with a swampy, musky smell, which at the time I did not realize came from the turtle. When I smelled it again in Maine, it did not specifically recall the physical scene—the turtle, the Marlowes, the dark little store. Instead, it brought back directly a sensation of alarm, confusion, and disorientation, in about the same way that the smell of anesthetic does not bring back the operating room so much as it brings back the vertiginous feeling of the self whirling away from itself.

The others came in right behind me. I was too mortified by my own embarrassment and disgrace to see how they reacted to the

~

whole scene, but I think they must have enjoyed it. It had been a good joke, to place the turtle just inside the threshold like that; if it had been played on anyone else, I would have laughed myself. Billy looked down at the turtle and said he'd never seen one that big. In the corner of the evil mouth, which was gaping open, was a big hook, with a piece of heavy line attached to it. "Caught him on a trotline, I see," said Billy.

Trotlines—a short length of line tied to a branch that over-hangs the water, so that the baited hook is just below the sur-face—were and are a common way of fishing, and they were perfectly legal for catching certain species of fish at certain times of year. But they were so widely used by poachers that to call a man a *trotliner* might, if the man were sufficiently thin-skinned, seem tantamount to an indictment. I don't know. I only know that when Billy said "trotline" the man in the chair gave him a sudden look and got up.

When he stood, he lurched and swayed, and we could see that he was ruinously drunk. He was wiry, short, and grizzled, wore knee-high rubber boots with the swamp mud still on them. He glared at Billy: "Your name ain't *McNair*, is it?" Billy said it wasn't and tried to ask the man if anything besides turtles had been biting that morning, but the man kept on; "You sure it ain't *McNair*? You sure you ain't some of them wildlife boys come down here? What you got that aerial on your truck for if you ain't?" He was right about at least that much. The company truck did have a two-way radio, and it was painted yellow, which gave it an official look, but it seemed not simply ridiculous but perverse for the man to take the four of us—hot, dirty, and dressed in ordinary work clothes—for some kind of undercover squad from the Department of Fish and Wildlife.

The man behind the counter told him to shut up and sit down, but he spoke in a half-hearted way, as though he knew it were useless. The boy in the back of the store, where I'd gone to get some crackers, had stopped sweeping and gone up to the front to watch the fun. The drunk man was telling Billy exactly what he'd do to McNair if McNair ever stuck his nose in here; he got louder and louder, and seemed to be working himself into the conviction that Billy really was McNair. I got my crackers and came up to the counter. It did not occur to me that anything serious was going on, and even if it was, there was no reason to worry. The drunk man's head scarcely came to Billy's shoulder. It seemed that all of this might in some way still be part of the joke; if not, it would make a good joke to tell, how Billy Watson, of all people, had been mistaken for a game warden.

I was paying for my crackers when the man said: "Let McNair come in here and I'll show him *this*," and I looked up and he had a pistol in his hand. It came from under the counter, as I later learned—the drunk man had reached over and grabbed it when the man behind the counter had turned to the cash register.

It changed everything; the world began to slip away. I had no impulse to act, and did not exactly feel fear. It was more an instinct to call out to everybody, to say *wait a minute; how did we get here? what's going on? let's talk this over and see if we can't make sense of it*. Billy's back was to me. The pistol was a snub-nosed revolver—a heavy, ugly, blunt thing. It was as though I could see through Billy's eyes the rounded noses of the cartridges in the open ends of the cylinders. Everything was utterly distinct and utterly unreal: we were under water, or had fallen asleep and were dreaming and were struggling mightily to waken ourselves from the dream before it reached the point it was meant to reach. Nobody moved to interfere. The thing was going to take its course.

The drunk man had the pistol right in Billy's face, shaking it. His own face was white with rage. "I'd show him *this*," he said, "and *this* is what I'd do with it." He reached down so abruptly and savagely that I winced, and he snatched the turtle by the tail and dragged it out the door, onto the concrete pad beside the gas pumps. The weight of the turtle was great; the man straightened himself slowly, as though only his wrath had enabled him to haul it this far. The turtle seemed weary, deflated, too long out of water. The man nudged its head with his boot, and the turtle hissed and struck feebly toward him. The man glared down at it, letting his rage recover and build back in him. He looked like a diver, gathering to plunge. The turtle's mouth hung open; when it hissed again the man's arm suddenly jerked down with the pistol and he shot it, shattering the turtle's head. "That's what I'd do to that goddamned McNair."

The man came back in and sat down heavily, spent, and the world returned to its ordinary focus. Blood had spattered onto the man's boot and pant leg. By the time we finished buying lunch and were ready to leave, he was snoring easily. The man behind the cash register told the boy to tote that thing off into the bushes, and the boy did, dragging the turtle by the tail, the blood still welling from the smashed head. When we got back to the truck I glanced over there, not wanting to, and could see the head swarming with flies, the big feet limp in the sand.

As we were getting into the truck, Wendell, who seldom said anything, said, "Well." We looked at him. He elaborated, his face perfectly deadpan: "Well. Good thing none of them *bad* Marlowes happened to be in today."

Hannah finished filling the hole, tamped the sand smooth, and brushed her palms briskly against each other, signifying that the job was done. The dog roused himself and we all walked back up toward the house. A yellow warbler flew across in front of us—a quick flash of color—perched on a willow branch, sang its hurried, wheezy song, and dropped from sight. Birdsong lasts longer into the morning on these cool, overcast days. The bobolinks were still busy about it, a song that sounds something like an audiotape being rewound at high speed. A robin in a clump of sumacs sang its careful phrase, as though for the edification of less gifted birds, then listened to itself a moment, head cocked appreciatively, then sang the phrase again. A meadowlark whistled from a fencepost. New England seemed, as it often does, more perfect in the intensity of its seasonal moment, and in the whole seasonal cycle that can be felt within the moment, than any place has a right to be. I felt the fatal parental urge, wanting to point out to Hannah all the richness that surrounded her. But to Hannah such familiar sights and sounds were equivalent to presuppositions, invisible until disturbed.

Animals fit themselves enigmatically into the secondary ecology of human thinking. "They are all beasts of burden, in a sense," says Thoreau, "made to carry some portion of our thoughts." Turtles are especially burdened. In Hindu myth, Vishnu, floating on the cosmic sea, takes the form of a tortoise and sustains the world on his back. North American Indians, unacquainted with any sizeable tortoises, nevertheless had the same myth of turtle as Atlas. The Senecans told how the first people lived in the sky, until a woman, whose transgression involved a tree, was thrown out. Below her—very far below—there was only water. A few water birds were there, and these, seeing her descending, hurried to prepare a place for her. They dived to the bottom, found mud and a turtle, and persuaded the turtle to let them place mud on its back, and make a dry spot for her to land on. The woman landed; vegetation grew up out of the mud; and the familiar world we know came into being.

But the Indians weren't through with the turtle, or vice versa. Turtle turns trickster and, disguised as a young brave, seduces the daughter of the first woman. When the daughter realizes what her lover is, she dies, and from her body, as she prophesies in dying, grow the first stalks of corn and the equivocal blessings of agriculture. Among other tribes, in other myths, Turtle continues his depredations. Many tribes tell of his going on the warpath against the first people, who at last catch him and prepare his death. They threaten him with fire; he tells them that he loves fire. They threaten him with boiling water; he begs to be put immediately into the kettle, because he so relishes being boiled. They threaten to throw

A Snapping Turtle in June

him into the river. "Anything but that," says Turtle, and so they throw him in. He sticks out his snout and laughs; they curse him and throw sticks, but he easily avoids them. And so Turtle takes up, one would surmise, the life of a snapper, coming ashore only briefly each year, seeming about as old as the earth, and spreading consternation. God knows what burden of thought the big snapper had borne for the drunk man at Yauhannah Bridge—he symbolized, I believe, a good deal more than the man's adversary, McNair.

I found myself wishing that Hannah had stumbled upon this morning's turtle herself and had confronted the potent oddity of the beast without having it all explained away for her. It might have stood a better chance then than it did now of becoming a fact in her imagination: something she would eventually remember and think about and think with from her days as a country girl. But what any child will think or remember is beyond anybody's knowing, including its own. The turtle had disappeared down the ditch; its hole had been filled. Meanwhile, Hannah let us know that we had on our hands a Tuesday morning in June, which was, with kindergarten over, a problem to be solved. Could she have a friend over? Could we go to town?

2 Of Moose and a Moose Hunter

When I first moved to Maine, I think I must have assumed that moose were pretty well extinct here, like the wolf or the caribou or the Abenaki Indian. But we had scarcely been in our house a week when a neighbor called us over to see one. She had a milk cow, and a yearling moose had developed a sort of fixation on it. The moose would come to the feedlot every afternoon at dusk and lean against the fence, moving along it when the cow did, staying as close to her as possible. Spectators made it skittish, and it would roll its eyes at us nervously and edge away from the lot, but never very far. It was gangly and ungainly; it held its head high, and had a loose, disjointed, herky-jerky trot that made it look like a puppet on a string.

The young moose hung around for a couple of weeks, and it became a small ritual to walk over in the summer evenings and watch it. My neighbor, Virginia Foster, had reported it to the warden, and the warden told her not to worry: the yearling had probably been driven off by its mother when the time had come for her to calve again, and it was just looking for a surrogate. It would soon give up and wander away, he said, and he was right. But until that happened, I felt that Susan and I, at the beginning of our own quasi-rural existence, were seeing something from the absolute beginnings of all rural existence—a wild creature, baffled and intrigued by the dazzling peculiarities of humankind, was tentatively coming forward as a candidate for domestication. Mrs. Foster said that if the moose planned to hang around and mooch hay all winter, he'd damn well better expect to find himself in the traces and pulling a plough come spring.

First encounters mean a lot, and in the years that followed, moose never became for me what they are for many people in Maine: the incarnation and outward projection of that sense of wilderness and wildness that is inside you, like an emotion. As soon as I began going up into the northern part of the state whenever I could, for canoeing and trout fishing, the sight of them came to be familiar and ordinary, hardly worth mentioning. You would see one browsing along the shoulder of a busy highway or standing unconcerned in a roadside bog, while cars stopped and people got out and pointed and shutters clicked. Driving out on a rough logging road at dusk, after a day of trout fishing, you would get behind one, and it would lunge down the road ahead of you. Not wanting to panic it or cause it to hurt itself—a running moose looks out of kilter and all akimbo, like a small boy trying to ride a large bicycle—you'd stop, to allow the moose to get around the next curve, compose itself, and step out of the road. Then you'd go forward, around the curve, and there would be the moose, standing and waiting for the car to catch up to it and scare it out of its wits again. Sometimes you could follow one for half a mile like that, the moose never losing its capacity for undiluted primal horror and amazement each time the car came into sight. Finally it would turn out of the road, stand at the fringe of the woods, and, looking stricken and crestfallen as a lost dog, watch you go past.

Of course you also see them in postcard situations: belly deep in a placid pond, against a backdrop of mountains and sunset, or wading across the upper Kennebec, effortlessly keeping their feet in tumbling water that would knock a man down. Once two of them, a bull and a cow, materialized in a duck marsh as dawn came, and I watched them change from dim, looming silhouettes that looked prehistoric, like something drawn by the flickering illuminations of firelight on the walls of a cave, into things of bulk and substance, the bull wonderfully dark coated and, with his wide sweep of antlers and powerfully humped shoulders, momentarily regal.

But even when enhanced by the vast and powerful landscape they inhabit, moose remained for me animals whose ultimate context was somehow pastoral. An eighteenth- or nineteenth-century English or American landscape painting, showing cattle drinking at dusk from a gleaming river, or standing patiently in the shade of an oak, conveys a serenity that is profound and profoundly fragile. The cattle look sacred, and we know that they are not. To the extent that they epitomize mildness, peace, and contentment, they, and the paintings in which they occur, tacitly remind us that our allegiance to such virtues is qualified and unenduring, existing in the context of our historical violence, our love of excitement, motion, risk, and change. When I would be hunting or fishing, and a moose would present itself, it would not seem to come out of the world of predator and prey, where grim Darwinian rules determine every action. That world and those rules allow the opposite ends of our experience to meet, connecting our conception of the city to our conception of the wilderness. The moose would seem to come from some place altogether different, and that place most resembled the elegiac world of the pastoral paint-

ing, an Arcadian daydream of man and nature harmoniously oblivious to the facts of man and nature.

I suppose it would be more accurate to say that the moose came
from wherever it came from, but that it seemed to enter the Arcadian region of the imagination. I found it a difficult animal to
respond to. It was obviously wild, but it utterly lacked the poised
alertness and magical evanescence that wild animals have. If by
good fortune you manage to see a deer or fox or coyote before it
sees you, and can watch it as it goes about its business unawares,
you hold your breath and count the seconds. There is the sensation of penetrating a deep privacy, and there is something of
Actaeon and Artemis in it—an illicit and dangerous joy in this
spying. The animal's momentary vulnerability, despite all its
watchfulness and wariness, brings your own life very close to the
surface. But when you see a moose, it is always unawares. It merely
looks peculiar, like something from very far away, a mild, dis-
placed creature that you might more reasonably expect to encoun-
ter in a zoo.

In 1980, for the first time in forty-five years, Maine declared an
open season on moose. Given the nature of the animal, this was
bound to be a controversial decision. People organized, circulated
petitions, collected signatures, and forced a special referendum.
There were televised debates, bumper stickers, advertising cam-
paigns, and letters to editors. The major newspapers took sides;
judicious politicians commissioned polls. One side proclaimed the
moose to be the state's sacred and official animal. The other side
proclaimed moose hunting to be an ancient and endangered heritage, threatened by officious interlopers who had no understanding of the state's traditional way of life. Each side accused the
other of being lavishly subsidized by alien organizations with sinister agendas: the Sierra Club, the National Rifle Association. The
argument assumed ideological overtones: doves *vs.* hawks; new-

comers *vs.* natives; urban Maine *vs.* rural Maine; liberals *vs.* conservatives.

At first this seemed to be just the usual rhetoric and rigmarole of public controversy. But as the debate continued, the moose seemed to become a test case for something never wholly articulated. It was as though we had to choose between simplified definitions of ourselves as a species. Moose hunters spoke in terms of our biology and our deep past. They maintained that we are predators, carnivores, of the earth earthly; that the killing and the eating of the moose expressed us as we always had been. The other side saw us as creatures compelled by civilization to evolve: to choose enlightenment over atavism, progress over regression, the hope of a gentler world to come over the legacy of instinctual violence. Both sides claimed the sanction of Nature—the moose hunters by embodying it, their opponents by protecting it. Each side dismissed the other's claim as sentimental nonsense.

I knew all along that when it came to moose hunting I was a prohibitionist, an abolitionist, a protectionist, but not a terribly zealous one. When the votes were counted and the attempt to repeal the moose season had been defeated, I doubted that much had been lost, in any practical way. The hunt was to last only a week, and only a thousand hunters, their names selected by lottery, would receive permits each year. It had been alleged that once moose were hunted, they would become as wild and wary as deer, but they have proved to be entirely ineducable. Hunter success ran close to 90 percent in that first year, and has been just as high in the years that followed; and the moose I continue to see each summer are no smarter or shyer than the one that had mooned around Mrs. Foster's feedlot, yearning to be adopted by her cow.

Late one afternoon, toward the end of September, the telephone rang, and there was a small voice, recognizably Terri Delisle's: "Liz there?" So I went and got Liz. She's old enough to have overcome all but the very last, genetically encoded traces of telephobia—just a momentary look of worry when she hears that it's for her, and a tentativeness in her "Hullo?" as though she were speaking not into the receiver but into a dark and possibly empty room.

Terri is her friend, her crony. The two of them get together— both polite, reticent, and normally quiet little girls—and spontaneously constitute between themselves a manic, exuberant subculture. It possesses them. They are no longer Terri and Liz but something collective: a swarm, a gang, a pack, or a carnival, having its own unruly gusts of volition. They glitter with mischief, laugh at everything, giggle, romp, and frolic; and I believe that, with each other's help, they actually lose for a moment all consciousness of the adult world that watches from within, waiting for children to draw toward it. They aren't destructive or insubordinate—that, after all, would be a backhanded acknowledgment of civilization, maturity, and responsibility. They are simply beyond the reach of reproof, like colts or puppies.

But on the telephone, with distance between them, self-conscious circumspection took over. I heard Liz's guarded and rigorously monosyllabic responses: "Yep." "He did?" "Sure—I'll have to ask Dad." "OK. Bye." And so she told me that Terri's father Henry had killed a moose. Would we like to go over and see it? "Sure," I say, all adult irony, "I'll have to ask Mom."

I knew Henry Delisle in a small and pleasant way. There were a lot of Delisles in town, and Henry, like his brother and most of his male cousins, worked over in Bath, at the shipyard—a welder, I think. But like many other natives of Bowdoinham, he had farming in the blood. The old Delisle farm, up on the Carding Machine Road, had long since been subdivided and sold, and Henry's neat, suburban-looking house sat on a wooded lot of only two or three acres. Even so, he had built himself a barn and a stock pen, and he kept a few pigs, a milk cow, and an old draft horse named Homer. There couldn't have been much economic sense to it, just a feeling that a house wasn't a home without livestock squealing or lowing or whickering out back. He plainly liked the whole life that livestock impose upon their owners—harnessing Homer up for a day of cutting and hauling firewood; making arrangements with local restaurants and grocery stores to get their spoiled and leftover food for pig fodder; getting the cow serviced every so often, and fattening the calf for the freezer. He had an antiquated Allis-Chalmers tractor, with a sickle bar and a tedder and a bailer. There are a lot of untended fields in Bowdoinham, and plenty of people were glad to let Henry have the hay if he would keep them mown.

That was how I had met him for the first time. He had come rattling up to the house in his big dilapidated flatbed truck to ask me if anybody planned to cut my fields that summer. In fact somebody did, and I told him so, but Henry had too much small-town civility, which coexists comfortably with small-town curiosity, simply to turn around and drive off. I appreciated that, and so we chatted for a while—Henry sitting up in his truck, talking with an abrupt and fidgety energy, and I standing down beside it.

He remembered my house from his boyhood: "Used to be a reg'lar old wreck of a place. They didn't have no electricity down here or nothing. Winters, they'd cut ice from the pond. Had a icehouse dug into the bank there; kept ice all through summer. Hard living." He told me a story I'd heard even before we bought the house, how one winter the eldest son had gone out to the barn to milk, as he did every morning, and had found his younger brother there, hanging from a ceiling joist. "Never a word or a note. That was a terrible thing to happen. Unfriendly people, but they didn't deserve that."

He laughed. "But they was *some* unfriendly, I want to tell you. I slipped down to the pond and set muskrat traps one fall. But they musta seen me. They pulled 'em every one out and kept 'em. I was afraid to ask—just a kid, you know. Probably still lying around in your barn somewhere." He looked at me and sized me up: "But I ain't afraid to ask now, and don't you be afraid to turn me down—

would you mind me setting a few traps in that pond this fall? It used to be about lousy with muskrats." I hesitated at this—the pond was still full of muskrats, and I enjoyed seeing them sculling across it, pushing little bundles of cut grass ahead of them, or sitting out on a log, grooming themselves with a quick, professional adroitness. But I liked him for the way he had asked it, and there was something else. His country-bred practicality and local knowledge gave him an obscure claim—he was less indigenous than the muskrats, but far more so than I was. "Sure," I told him, "go ahead."

All this had taken place on a bright, airy morning in late July or early August, with the kind of high sky that would make anybody think of haying. Henry said he was glad he'd stopped by, and that I'd see him again once the trapping season opened. I reached up; we shook hands, and he backed the truck down the driveway. His windshield caught the sun for a moment and blinded me and then, as the truck swung up into the yard to turn around, I could see through the glass what I had not been able to see before. He had a passenger—a little girl sitting in the middle of the seat, right at his elbow. She did not look in my direction at all, but stared at the dashboard with that look of vacancy and suspended animation that you see on the faces of children watching Saturday morning cartoons. Henry grinned at me, waved goodbye, and the big truck went lumbering off.

That first meeting with Henry had been the summer before Elizabeth and Terri started school. Later, when they had become classmates and best friends, I learned that the girl I had seen in the truck was Stephanie, whom everybody called Tadpole. She was three years older than Terri, but that was a technicality.

Bowdoinham is a small, spread-out town. It tries to hold onto the idealized ethos of the New England village, but is in fact well on its way to becoming a bedroom community, a pucker-brush suburb. Like the state as a whole, it is full of outsiders moving in, old-timers dying out, and the uneasy sense of a lost distinctiveness.

The elementary school is the nearest thing to an agora that such a town has. Parents are separated by their backgrounds and expectations, and by the devious anxieties of people who feel that, in appearing to belong to the little unglamorous place they inhabit, they may misrepresent or compromise themselves. But children go to school, and it stands for the world. They make friends and enemies, and suddenly populate your household with unfamiliar names. It is as though you had sent them off as members and worshipers of a stable, self-sufficient Trinity consisting of Mama, Daddy, and themselves; and then had them return as rampant polytheists, blissfully rejoicing or wailing despairingly about the favors and sulks of capricious gods and goddesses named Tommy Blanchard, Vera Sedgely, Joanie Dinsmore, Nikki Toothacre, and Willie Billings. At school functions you would meet the parents of these entities, or, prodded by your child, would nervously call up Joan's or Nikki's mom, and arrange for that child to come over and play. And slowly, with no direct intention of doing so, you would find out about other families in the town—who they were and how they lived, how they regarded themselves and how they were regarded.

So we learned that Tadpole suffered from Down's syndrome. She was the first child of Henry and Debbie Delisle, born to them within a year of their marriage, when they themselves were just out of high school. Perhaps if they had had more education and experience they would have accepted the irremediable fact of their daughter's condition. As it was, they were mistrustful of the state and the school system and all the experts who came to help them and warn them and in some way to deprive them of the right to raise their daughter as they saw fit. Against every recommendation, they were determined to try to give Tadpole all the circumstances of an ordinary childhood.

When time came for Tadpole to go to school, Henry wrangled

with the school board and the superintendent and the Department of Mental Health and Retardation. And finally everybody agreed that, for as long as it didn't create any disturbance, Tadpole could go to school with Terri. Word of that sort of thing gets around, and some parents didn't like it, fearing that what Henry had gained for his daughter would diminish the education and attention that their own children would receive. But I believe that most of us admired Henry and wished him well. He was his own man; in his battered old truck, with a tottering load of hay on it, or with Homer tethered to the headboard, he implied an old-fashioned resourcefulness and independence, which we could praise even if we couldn't emulate. It was heartening to see a man like that acting out of the best and simplest human impulse, and sticking to his guns, even if, in the long run, the case were hopeless.

And of course the case was hopeless, although at first it didn't appear to be. Tadpole was docile and affectionate, and in her first year and a half of school, she enjoyed an almost privileged status among her classmates. It was as though she were their mascot, like the wheezy old bulldog or jessed eagle you might find on the sidelines at a college football game. You would see a crowd of children fussing over her in the schoolyard, alternately courting her as though she were a potentate to be appeased, or babying her with bossy solicitude. Liz would report on all that Tadpole had done or said, as though she were a celebrity, in whom we should take a communal pride. And we did take a kind of pride in her. Her being at the school with the other children seemed proof that humane flexibility, sympathy, and tolerance were still operative in this overgrown country. There was something quaint about it, something from the putative innocence of the past.

But by the end of the second grade, Liz was bringing home bad news. Tadpole had begun to balk at going to school, and would misbehave when she was there. She was bigger than her classmates, and her truculence threatened them. They retaliated as children would, by teasing and persecution. She regressed, growing more withdrawn and morose, and would go through days of not speaking, or of only muttering to herself. Public opinion hardened. I don't think there were any petitions or formal proceedings to have Tadpole removed; it was just one of those sad things that had become plain and obvious. Henry and Debbie had no choice; they had to give in to the fact that confronted them every day. The next year, Tadpole and Terri were separated, and Tadpole was sent to school in Topsham, where there was a class for what the state calls Special Children.

When Terri would come over to play, she seemed untroubled by the change. She was as quick and inventive as ever. I did not know Henry well enough or see him often enough to speak to him about the matter, and hardly knew what I would or could have said. He got himself transferred to the night shift at the shipyard that fall, and he must have kept Tadpole out of the special class a good deal. I would regularly see the two of them together in the truck—usually first thing in the morning, when he'd just gotten off work. But he told me one morning, when he'd come to check the muskrat traps, that he had changed shifts purely to give himself more time for the woodcutting, haying, trapping, ice-fishing, and hunting that seemed to be his natural vocations.

So on the September afternoon in question, Liz and I got into the car—none of the rest of the household had any interest in a dead moose—and drove over. It was nearly dark when we turned up into Henry's driveway. His garage lights were on. He had set up a worktable of planks and sawhorses along the rear wall; the moose was hanging by the neck squarely in the center of the garage. From the driveway, it looked like a shrine or a crèche—the brightly lit space, clean and spare as an Edward Hopper interior; Henry and four other men standing chatting; and, just behind them, the lynched moose. Terri came running out, excited as on Christmas morning, and took us in to see.

Of Moose and a Moose Hunter

From the outside, the moose's head appeared to go right up through the low ceiling of the garage, but once inside I could see that, when he had built the garage, Henry had left out one four-by-eight ceiling panel, to give him access to the attic. He had put an eye bolt in a collar tie, centered above the opening, so that he could rig a hoist from it. It was a smart arrangement, enabling him to convert an ordinary two-car garage into an abattoir whenever he had a cow or pig or deer to slaughter. The moose he had shot was a cow, and she was a big animal, hanging with her head in the attic, her rump scarcely a foot above the concrete floor. A big animal but not, Henry said, a big moose: "She'll dress out about five-fifty. Just a heifer. She'd have calved next spring."

Henry introduced me to the other men—neighbors who had wandered over out of curiosity, and his cousin Paul, who had been his partner in the hunt.

We were somehow an uncomfortably self-conscious group; it was as though we were all trying to ignore something. Perhaps it was that Paul and Henry were still dressed in their stained and ragged hunting gear, and were grubby and unshaven. The rest of us were in our ordinary street clothes, and only a few minutes ago were watching television or pottering around the house or having a drink and getting ready for supper. We had been in our familiar cocoons of routine and obligation, where the only world that matters is the human one. And now we were talking to men who were in another role, and we were abruptly confronting a large, dead animal, a thing from far beyond our lives.

I think it was more this awkwardness than aggression that made the man next to me, a bank manager new to town, speak the way he did: "Well, Henry. That's a weird damned animal. You sure it's not a camel?" Everybody laughed, but uneasily.

"Tell us about it," the man said. "How'd you bag the wily moose?"

Henry said there wasn't a whole lot to tell. The man asked him if he'd hired a guide. Henry said he hadn't.

"Well maybe you should have," the bank manager said. "If you had, you might have gotten yourself a bull. Then you'd have something to hang in your den."

Henry didn't answer. He got busy with a knife, whetting it against a butcher's steel. The man walked around the moose, looking at her appraisingly, as though she were an item in a yard sale. Then he said he had to get on back home, and left, and there was a general relaxing. Henry looked up.

Now he was going to tell us how you kill a moose, or how he had killed this one. None of us knew anything about moose hunting. The tradition of it had died out, and hunters—even very experienced ones like Henry and Paul—don't know moose in the way that they know deer. The hunt was limited to the upper third of the state, and a lot of people up there had set themselves up as moose guides, offering what was supposedly their deep-woods wisdom to anybody lucky enough to have a permit.

Henry snorted: "Hire a guide. You know what a moose guide is? He's a guy with a skidder, that's all. You go to his house and he'll take you out and leave you somewheres where he thinks there might be a moose, and charge you so much for that. Then you kill a moose and he'll charge you a arm and a leg to hook it up to the skidder and drag it out to your truck. So I go to this guy that's listed as a guide, and he explains it to me. And I say to him, 'Look. Don't tell me a word about where to find a moose. Now if I get one, what'll you charge to drag him out?' 'Hundred dollars for the first hour; fifty dollars per hour after that,' he says. See, they got you. Law don't let you kill a moose less than fifty yards from the road. So I says to him, 'You prorate that first hour?' 'Fifty dollar minimum,' he says to me: 'Take it or leave it.' Musta thought I was from Massachusetts. 'See you later,' I says. And that fifty dollar, hundred dollar shit ain't from the time he drives his skidder off his trailer into the woods. It's from the time he gets in his truck right there in his front yard."

Paul quietly removed himself from Henry's audience and went

into the kitchen. It wasn't his story, and there was a lot of work still to do.

"We had topo maps, and I seen some good bogs. Day before the season opened we drove and scouted all day. I don't know much about moose, but I know a moose'll walk on a log road or a skidder track if he can, instead of bustin' through the bushes. About suppertime we see a cow cross the road ahead of us, and go down a skidder trail. We followed her down on foot. There was a bog in there at the end of the trail, about a quarter mile in off the road, and there she was, feeding. Her and another cow too. That skidder trail was rough, but I figured we might be able to get the truck down it.

"Opening day it was raining. We parked a ways off and walked up to the skidder track and down to the bog. Got there before day. When it come day, one cow was there. I looked at her. She looked good, but not extra good. Animal like a moose got a lot of waste on 'em. Big bones, big body cavity—not as much meat as you'd think. That's what they tell me. And they told me when you see a cow, wait. It's rut, and a big bull might come along any time."

Paul came out from the house with his arms full—wrapping paper, freezer tape, a roll of builder's plastic. He spread the plastic over the table, and he didn't make any effort to be unobtrusive about it. But Henry was occupied by his story. It was like something he wanted to get off his chest or conscience. Maybe he just couldn't get over the strangeness of the moose.

"It ain't like a deer. A cow moose calls a bull. That's what they say and it's the truth. We watched her all day, and ever so often she'd set right down on her butt and beller, like a cow that ain't been milked. So we set there too, and waited, but no bull showed. By dark she'd worked over to the other side of the bog. Shoot her there and you'd have to cut her up and pack her out."

Henry was standing in front of the moose. Her chin was elevated and her long-lashed eyes were closed. All of the things that had so splendidly adapted her to her world of boreal forest, bog, and swamp made her look grotesque here: the great hollow snout, the splayed feet and overlong, knob-kneed legs. In whatever consciousness she had had, it was still the Ice Age—she was incapable of grasping human purposes or adjusting to human proximity. Her death was almost the first ritual of civilization, yet she was in our present, suspended in the naked light of a suburban garage, and we could only stand, hands in pockets, as though it were something we did every day.

"So we come back the next day, a little earlier even, and I sent Paul around to the far side of the bog. This time I hear her walking in on that skidder track just before day, and she got out in the bog and bellered some more. We was going to give her 'til noon. I figured if a bull showed, he'd come up the track too, and I could get him before he hit the bog.

"By noon she was all the way out in the middle of the bog again, but Paul stepped out of the bushes, easy, so's not to scare her too much. Took her the longest time even to notice him. Then she started trotting toward me, but she'd keep stopping to beller some more. It was almost like she was mad."

One of the men chuckled: "More like she was desperate, if you ask me. If she didn't call herself up a boyfriend pretty quick, she was a dead duck."

"Well. Anyway, Paul had to slog out after her, keep shooing her along. I wanted her to get all the way out on the trail, but she musta smelt me. Stopped about ten foot from the woods and started throwing her head around and acting jumpy, like she might bolt. So I shot her there.

"We had a little work with the chain saw to clear the skidder trail out wide enough for the truck. Then we backed in and put a rope around her and dragged her out to dry ground. Used a come-along to hoist her up on a tree limb and dressed her out right there. Then cranked her up some more, backed the truck under, and lowered her in. On the way out, we stopped by that guy's house. I went in and told him we wouldn't be needing his damn skidder this year."

The whole time Henry talked, Paul kept coming and going, bringing out knives, a cleaver, a meat saw, and a plastic tarp. Elizabeth and Terri had examined the moose and then gone inside. I had been worried about Elizabeth. She was at least as sentimental as the average ten-year-old about animals; at country fairs she would lean against the stalls and gaze with pure yearning at Suffolk sheep or Highland cattle and especially at horses of any description. But she and Terri had looked the moose over as though she were a display in a museum of natural history, something interesting but remote. They had walked around her, rubbed the coarse, stiff hair, and inspected the big cloven feet, and then gone about their business.

Now, as Henry finished his story, they returned, giggling. Terri was carrying a child's chair, and Liz looked from her to me, trying not to laugh. Terri ran up to the moose and slipped the chair under her rump, and then the two of them stood back and waited on our reaction.

It was comic relief or comic desecration. Because the moose's hindquarters were so near the floor, her hind legs were spread stiffly out in front of her. With the addition of the chair, you suddenly saw her in a human posture, or really in two human postures. From the waist down, she looked like a big man sprawled back on a low seat. Above the waist, she had the posture of a well-bred lady of the old school, her back very straight, her head aloof, and her whole figure suggesting a strenuous and anxious rectitude.

In the ready, makeshift way of country people, Henry had taken one of Debbie's old worn-out lace curtains with him, and when he had killed and cleaned the moose, he had pinned the curtain across the body cavity, to keep out debris and insects and to allow the air to circulate and cool the animal while he and Paul drove back home. The curtain was longer than it needed to be, and now

Terri picked up one end of it, brought it like a diaper up between the moose's legs, wrapped it around the hips, and tucked it in, so that it would stay up. The effect was funny in a way I don't like to admit I saw—the garment looked like something between a pinafore and a tutu. It was as though the moose had decided, in some moment of splendid delusion, to take up tap dancing or ballet, and was now waiting uncomfortably to go on stage for her first recital.

Terri and Liz admired the moose. "She needs a hat," Terri pronounced, and they ducked into the house. What they came out with was better than a hat—a coronet of plastic flowers, left over from some beauty pageant or costume.

"Daddy, could you put this on her? She's too high for us."

She was too high for Henry too, but he pulled the little chair from beneath the moose, then picked Terri up and set her on his shoulders. He stood on the chair and Terri, leaning out daringly, like a painter on a stepladder, managed to loop the coronet over one of the long ears, so that it hung lopsided. She slid down Henry to the ground, stepped back and dusted her hands together:

"There. That'll just have to do. I think Momma needs to see this. Maybe she'll lend us some mittens and a scarf. Let's go get her and Tadpole to come see."

"Terri, Paul and me got to get to work on that moose right now," Henry called after her, but she was already gone. The other two men who had come over to see the moose said they had to go, and left, one on foot and one in his car. Terri and Liz came back out with Debbie and Tadpole. Debbie looked at the moose and laughed. Terri was pleased.

"Don't you think she looks like a beauty queen, Mom? We could enter her in the Miss Bowdoinham contest."

"Well I guess so." Debbie turned to Tadpole: "Look at Daddy's moose that he brought us, honey." Tadpole looked at it and walked over as though she wanted to touch it, but didn't. Her face had that puffy, numbed look of someone just wakened from a deep sleep, and her movements were slow and labored.

Debbie called over to Terri. "Now your Daddy and Paul have to start, and I've got to run buy some more freezer paper. You and Stephanie come with me, and we can let Liz get home for her supper."

Terri gave the moose a comradely whack on the rump: "Good-bye, moose. You're going in the freezer." Liz patted the moose too, but more tentatively. Then they all trooped out.

I stood talking to Henry for a few minutes longer. He looked at the moose with her cockeyed halo and tried to make a joke of it. "If she'd been dressed that way this morning, maybe I'd have got a bull." But his laughter was awkward, apologetic. His remark about how little useable meat there really was on a moose, for all its great size, had not been lost on me, and yet I felt that it would be right to ask him for something, as a way of restoring to him a vestige of the old role of hunter as public benefactor, bringer home of the bacon. So I asked him if I could have some of the long hair from the nape of her neck, for trout flies.

"Sure thing," he said, all business. "Tell you what: I won't cut it off now—don't want no more loose hair than I can help when we go to skin her. But when she's done, I'll clip some off and drop it by, next time I'm down your way. You can count on it."

I thanked him and left. Liz was subdued as we drove back toward home. You might have asked an older child what she was thinking, but not Liz, not for a few years yet. Besides, I wasn't so certain what *I* was thinking just then: two scenes alternated in my mind. One was a recollection, back from the previous November, a morning when heavy frost had sparkled white as mica on the dead grass, and I had been driving to work. I saw Henry walking across a stubble field, a big fox slung over his shoulder. He held the fox by its hind legs; its tail, curved over and lying along its back, was luxuriant and soft as an ostrich plume, and it stirred lightly in the breeze. I felt some sadness for the dead beauty of the fox, but it was Henry I remembered. He ought to have looked like a mighty hunter before the Lord, holding the bounty of his skill and cunning and knowledge of the ways of wild animals in his hand. But he was walking with a shambling hesitation, to keep pace with the daughter clinging to his other hand and trudging glumly at his side, beyond any idea of triumph or happiness.

The other image was of something that had not happened yet. June would come again, and I would be up north fishing again— this time with a fly that would have, wrapped in tight spirals around the shank of the hook to imitate the segmented body of a nymph or mayfly, one or two strands of mane from Henry's moose. And I would look up from the water, almost dizzy with staring for so long at nothing but the tiny fly drifting in the current, and there they would be—maybe a cow and a calf—standing on the other bank, watching me watch them, trying to fathom it.

3 In a Small Pond

Nick Adams got down from the train, shouldered his pack, and headed out across the scorched land, knowing he would strike the river further upstream. There he would make camp, and fish for trout. Reading and re-reading "Big Two-Hearted River" was a regular occupation of my boyhood. Daddy had a copy of *The Fifth Column and the First Forty-Nine Stories.* I do not know how young I was when I first took it down, read around in it, and found this story, which is not only Hemingway's best, the one that lies closest to the secret of his style, but is also the model for all fishing stories, and so for fishermen themselves, as they try to concentrate wholly on the subject at hand, putting their lives aside to wait on the strike that seldom comes.

It always seemed to be somewhere in the middle of a summer afternoon. Floors being cooler than rugs or beds, I would lie on the floor in front of an oscillating fan, its breeze passing over me, going away, hesitating at the end of its arc, returning. Nick Adams had it hot too, as he plodded with his heavy pack across the fire-scarred Michigan countryside; but when he got beyond the first low range of hills, he would enter groves of jackpine—a clean, open forest easy to imagine, although unlike any woodland I had ever seen—and there the air was fragrant with the sweetfern that he crushed beneath his boots as he walked. And when he reached the Big Two-Hearted River it ran cold and clear, and he could lay his burden down.

Outside, cane poles were stashed under the eaves of the garage. A ten-minute walk would take me down to Dargan's Landing, where I could sit in the stern of a wooden boat chained to a cypress and fish. There would be at least an earthy dankness, if not a coolness, and there would be the mystery of black, velvety water. All fishing solicits that mystery. But, if I were to fish, I would first need to scare up bait of some description, which was no easy job in midsummer, with every living creature lying low, shrinking its life down into a nook or recess like some one of those desert animals that go comatose until the rains evoke them, make them spring up like flowers. And I knew that by the time I got to Dargan's Landing, the dream of fishing would have begun to scale itself down to meagre possibilities—one or two bream, so tiny as to be translucent; perhaps a roach, useful only as live bait, or a small catfish, not even useful for that. Better to lie low myself, and start over again, with Nick now pausing at the railroad bridge to watch the trout in the big pool below him. They held themselves against the current, or shifted position in the stream, rose quickly to take an insect from the surface, then drifted back down, their shadows clearly visible on the gravel bottom, and resumed their stations. Watching them, Nick felt his heart tighten with the old happiness.

I was too young to recognize that his story was about a cleansing and healing of the spirit, but even a twelve-year-old boy could feel invited by its clear depths. So I would relapse into the Upper Peninsula, making it my refuge for another empty summer afternoon, while the fan hummed and the cicadas outside buzzed their parched, whetstone song, lapping and overlapping itself in slow waves, until at last dusk fell, a faint coolness seeped out from the grass, and the toads and crickets took over.

Daddy no more than I had what would have been Nick Adams's experience of fishing for trout from boyhood on up. Their cold rivers and deep blue lakes were worlds away from the Carolina lowcountry. Once or twice, when he was little, his mother had taken him and his brother to western North Carolina, to visit some family connection or other. It would have been a slow trip in those days, first through the flat, familiar country of pine woods and small farms, sunshine glinting off the tin roofs of tobacco barns; then the groundswell of the piedmont, sandhills giving way to red clay in rising undulations, distances revealed by elevation; and finally mountains, far-off and blue and hazy like low clouds or the ramparts of a visionary city, but drawing closer, becoming solid and real. The train labored up rocky grades; your ears felt funny inside, the air smelled like just after a thunderstorm, and an unfamiliar vegetation—hemlock, white pine, rhododendron, laurel—crowded in against the tracks. The towns were cramped, the houses jammed together and set close to the street. And there were headlong, foaming rivers, and local people who spoke about fishing in them. Perhaps that is where Daddy first heard about trout, or perhaps even already in his boyhood, as certainly in mine, no fisherman could recall a time when he had not known about trout and trout fishing, any more than a boy who owned a ball and bat could remember when he had first heard of Williams and Dimaggio, or Ruth and Gehrig.

When he married, Daddy took his bride back to that high country for their honeymoon. You must live in a hot, swampy, tidewater sort of a place to know the allure of mountains, to understand the psalmist: *I will lift up mine eyes unto the hills, from whence cometh my salvation.* People in Conway put themselves to some trouble, trying to grow laurel or rhododendron or flowering crab, as though those shrubs could elevate the town, make it faintly alpine in character. So nothing was unusual or suspect about my parents taking their honeymoon where they did. But Daddy had further plans: they would go up into Linville Gorge, where they would camp beside the Linville River. Nick Adams *à deux*. Or, as it turned out, *à trois*.

They hired a local man to guide them, Mr. Denny. They camped. Daddy and Mr. Denny fished in the river. And it rained, as Mama says, ev-e-ry bles-séd day. They had one small tent. Mr. Denny offered to sleep outside. Of course Mama and Daddy would not hear of it—they might have been honeymooners, but they were also Christians. If they hadn't been, I doubt that their marriage would have lasted, and it has lasted long enough now for Mama's honeymoon to have become a comic story; she speaks of Mr. Denny with the fondness that we can feel for what we have survived: "He was a reg'lar mountain man. A lanky old thing with a slouch hat and a beard down to his belt buckle. Your father says he doesn't remember it, but he told us he liked to bathe punctually—PUNCtually!—every Fourth of July, when the river had warmed up good. Never took his overalls off even then. Probably not his hat either. And, honey, this was May. When he crawled into that tent at night, with everything being damp and all, it smelt exactly like a pen full of billy goats."

I was not interested in that part of the story. The thing was, that Daddy and Mr. Denny fished in the river, and they caught fish, too: chub, warty little tadpole-looking things called horneyheads, dace, and rainbow trout. Two rainbow trout, in fact. There is a photograph, sepia-tinted the way the world was back then, so that even the rocks and shrubs look quaint and frail with antiquity; in it, my father-to-be holds the two trout aloft, one on the little finger of each hand. Mama provides the caption, spreading her thumb and forefinger apart, then drawing them together slightly, with micrometric precision: "About this big. In other words, just about the size of a sardine. And I mean your true Norwegian sardine, not that old sorry overgrown kind you wouldn't feed to a cat."

But it was not discouraging to me. Daddy had been there; he had caught trout, proving that they were not merely metaphorical or historical and extinct, like so many of the things that childhood tries to build on. And he said a big one had whirled up out of a deep pool, and flashed a silver flank behind his spinner. He cast for it again and again, on that day and the days that followed, but it never came back. When he left and returned to Conway and the life of a paterfamilias and breadwinner that awaited him, the trout was still there, a memory beside a rock down in Linville Gorge, growing.

On his own ground, he was a fine fisherman. He had started the way every boy in a small town like Conway would have started—a cane pole, a line made from his mother's sewing thread, platted together for strength, a few precious hooks, split shot, and an abundance of unprogrammed time. He explored the river landings, fished from old docks and half-sunken log rafts, the trestle over Kingston Lake, until he was old enough to get a paddling boat, and finally a car, and acquaint himself with the Waccamaw River from almost the North Carolina line right down to Winyah Bay. He saw and remembered things, and now at eighty can still point out a row of pilings in an unpromising backwater just above Grissett's Landing, where fifty years ago he had idly cast the plug, and something had taken it and headed downriver, never showing itself, breaking the line without even pausing or seeming to notice.

You treasure knowledge as a fisherman, and want to pass it on. Fishing alone, Nick Adams becomes autodidactic; we all do: "The very biggest ones would lie up close to the bank," he tells himself. "You could always pick them up there on the Black. When the sun was down they all moved out into the current. Just when the sun made the water blinding in the glare before it went down, you were liable to strike a big trout anywhere in the current." Izaac Walton casts himself as Piscator, the master of the art, but also as

Venator, the grateful and eager novice. Daddy passed on to me as much as he could, and I am grateful for it, even though much of the knowledge has now reached a dead end. I no longer have any practical need to know (and I doubt that you do) that, when you come across the tops and branches of felled pines, you should stop and listen for a low grating and grinding. If you hear it, get a hatchet, split off the bark, and you will find sapworms, a tough, forcep-mouthed grub that is the best bait of all for redbreast. If you notice an elongated, caramel-tan, and furtive bird frequenting a water oak, investigate. He is a cuckoo, and feeds ravenously on oakworms, a medium-sized caterpillar loved by bream and warmouth. You can shake down a week's supply of bait in half an hour. These are vestiges of a country competence, and I am proud to possess them; any real fisherman knows his business from the bottom up, and would feel himself less a fisherman if obligated to buy his bait—why not just buy the fish too?

So Daddy taught me the local lore and the local style of fishing, and my development as a fisherman in many ways recapitulated his. It was a serious and exacting business, requiring diligence, stealth, observation, and some dexterity. He was not patient with my blunders. The important thing was not to have a good time. It was to become a good fisherman, to go from being an apprentice to being a full partner in the enterprise. And, for a good fisherman, the object was not to bring home a mess of fish. It was to fish well, making no fuss or commotion; to savor the silent afternoons without much comment. In the beginning, we used only the throwline: a light and springy cane pole, twelve or fifteen feet long, with a length of monofilament line a foot or two longer than the pole; a small, cigar-shaped cork; and a long-shanked #10 hook. With some local variation, this is basic, universal, and immemorial equipment, not very far from the greenthorn or ash poles and braided horsehair lines that Walton would have used. Almost anybody, almost anywhere, who ever saw a throwline would know how to use it, and yet the effective use of it took skill and practice.

Looking back at it now, I can see the charm and beauty of fishing with the throwline. One of us managed the boat, keeping twenty or thirty feet from shore, usually back-paddling, lowering the boat slowly down the current; the other fished. The poles were brightly varnished, pale blond cane stippled and mottled with brown. Their pattern was less regular than the reticulated shadings of brown on the back of a water snake or moccasin, but it seemed equally intrinsic to the filtered and scattered light of the riverbank. And the rhythm of casting and waiting, watching the cork, then picking up with a smooth, deliberate sweep of the pole, casting again, gently, with no breaking of the wrist to cause the line to snap forward too quickly and throw the bait off the hook—that rhythm kept time with the pace of the river and the afternoon, unhurried and unemphatic as the desultory conversation, the occasional, strangely cavernous echo of the paddle thumping against the gunwale. All the drama lay in the least significant thing—the cork as it plopped into the water and sat there, time and again. Finally it would twitch or tremble, slide off across the water or cock itself up on one end and then slip beneath the surface, down and down, and you would lift the pole and tighten on a stiff, resistant, unknown life struggling against your own. In that first moment of feeling it, it might be anything.

The river air would take on a musty smell, like a newly ploughed field or a cellar, as the sun went below the trees. When the shadows reached from bank to bank, there was a strange, soft, moist edge of chill, something that registered more in your bones than against your skin. The first bats and mosquitoes came out, and I would begin to feel shivery and small, ready to call it quits, although never ready to say so. Daddy would say to take one more cast, and I would, and would watch the cork fervently, hoping for some final miracle of a fish. He would turn, fit the starter cord to its notch and wrap it around the flywheel. There was still time. A good deal of childhood is trying to prolong things, trying to fore-stall by will, prayer, superstition, or dawdling the processes that move toward the moment, to realize it and take it away. Daddy was deliberate, giving the fish every chance. He would open the air vent on top of the gas tank and the fuel valve underneath it, adjust the mixture to maximum richness, jiggle the float valve (this releasing the sharp, evocative smell of gasoline into the evening air), advance the spark, pause. And that would be it. I would lift the pole, unbait the hook, wrap the line around the pole, and carefully lay it down. Then Daddy would yank the cord. Never in its long life did the little one-lung Elto-Evinrude motor start on the first pull; never did it fail to start eventually, with a catch, a cough, a stutter. Then we could relax. On the way back to the landing, I could twist around on the front seat, open the lid of the fishbox, see water sloshing around inside, and the fish—mysteri-ous, insubstantial-looking, like images on a strip of undeveloped film—poised in the water, feather-edged gills working, pectorals fanning, bodies taut as a drawn bow. Even in the fishbox, in water not four inches deep, they were hard to see, and looked like birds' shadows that had been caught and detained, but might not be there when you looked again.

When I have dreams about fish and fishing now, there is always something wrong. The fish is malformed or diseased, or, although it is large, it is sluggish and limp, or comes out of some vile water—a ditch or sour puddle. The dream only seems to remind me, when I wake from it, of how the reality of fishing itself has become better than anything originating in my own mind. I don't mean in terms of fish caught, but in terms of a world encountered, absorbed, and absorbing. It doesn't need to aim at an end very far beyond itself. But I was bookish and introverted as a boy, lived more in theory than among facts, and always waited on a time when my circumstances would at last conform to what was prescribed by authors, and deliver me from an identity which, whether measured against my own standards, or against the modest and sensible expectations of my parents, was ignominious. I read all about fishing: fishing for tarpon in the Florida mangrove swamps; marlin and sailfish in the Gulf Stream; striped bass off Martha's Vineyard; muskie in the Chippewa flowage; Atlantic salmon on the Miramachi. But always trout loomed above everything else, as though their ontological status were definitive, the ratifying reality behind all piscatorial endeavor. All other angling could be judged by how closely its ambience and technique approximated trout fishing. The throwline, the cork, and a cricket or caterpillar on the hook came to seem too much like what I feared my life would be—something local, undistinguished, and limited, beneath the notice of literature and without shape or certification.

I learned to use the casting rod and the flyrod, and tried hard to make my fishing for redbreast and bonnet bream into something more than what it was. It was as though I were fishing in two places at once—the Waccamaw and also one of the far-famed rivers I read about over and over, until they grew legendary and floated free from terrestrial geography, like the Tigris and the Euphrates, or the Nile, or the River Dan and the River of Jordan. Their names were no less potent—Beaverkill and Battenkill; Ausable, Neversink, Letort; the Snake, the Madison; in England, the Dove, the Itchen, and the Test.

I came to favor light lines and small lures, especially ones that floated like the dry flies that, according to my readings in *Outdoor Life* and *Field and Stream*, trout fishermen used. The authorities stressed that the dry fly ought to be allowed to drift quietly with the current, and not be yanked or twitched, trout being highly skittish of anything that looked like unnatural behavior on the part of their prospective entrée. And so I would fish my bass bugs and bass plugs that way, although I knew from the same authorities, and even from some experience, that bass could often be provoked into striking a lure that was popped or jerked or skittered across the surface. But I reasoned that somewhere my redemption

and vindication lay in the form of an old bass, a huge and high-
minded fish that hearkened back to a bygone age when things had
been as they should be, commensurate with dreams and theories,
and that he would honor my truer art and austere purity of technique by striking a plug that was allowed to drift past a cypress
stump like a royal coachman—a red, green, white, and tan trout
fly of approved design—past a boulder in a mountain stream. I
caught the occasional small one that way, as was fitting—youth
and inexperience, suckers for theory, on both ends of the line—
but the best bass I ever caught came after I had let the plug float
along like the royal coachman, then given up on the cast and
begun cranking it in. As the plug burbled and spluttered back
toward the boat, kicking up a wake like an eggbeater and looking
like nothing condoned by nature or *Sports Afield,* the fish smashed
into it. It was gratifying to catch a good one, but disillusioning
too: somehow comparable to my discovery, quite a lot later, that
women also had sexual appetites and were not necessarily gratified
or impressed by one's endless, chivalrous, scrupulous restraint.

Daddy was of course more realistic and more successful, but he
could not entirely escape the archetype of trout fishing. He owned
a flyrod and taught me to use it, and he would often fish with it
himself, even though flyrods were less suited than cane poles to
the kind of fishing we did. And I learned from him that the best
fishing was on the upper Waccamaw, where the river was shallow
and flowed over white sandbars with a quick, live current, and the
water was black and clean. There were more and larger fish downstream, where the river slowed down, became tidal, and spread
out into swamps. But upriver was better for light tackle, easier to
imagine that, with only a little alteration, you might be on a trout
river. The fish here would be mostly bass and redbreast—active,
wholesome creatures. There were few of the primitive, voracious,
unspeakable mudfish (a. k. a. bowfin, grindle) that inhabited the
lower river, where they could at any time barge into your fisherman's idyll like a bunch of roughnecks into some local lady's attempt

at a cotillion or tea party. However much Daddy and I might have been pleased by the idea of the rowdies putting their brogans up on the tablecloth and using the fingerbowls for spittoons, we neither one of us saw any humor at all in a big mudfish's grabbing the plug and wallowing and rolling and thrashing, as they do when hooked, until at last you get them into the boat and try to get the hooks out of their leathery mouths while they writhe and twist and batter the floorboards until they've wrapped themselves hopelessly in the line, gotten a vile slime over everything they touch, and bent the hooks and mangled the plug to such an extent that at last, with a curse, you abandon gentility and a good deal of tackle, and heave them overboard. Local folklore said they came ashore on moonless nights, and molested goats.

Relatively safe on the upper river, we would drift along, one paddling while the other fished. We would generally wind up using the throwline more than anything else, but we would start with the flyrod, and sometimes, if nothing seemed to be biting anyway, would stay with it for the whole afternoon. The chief result of this was that, when I got to Maine and found myself in reach of that wonderful country where boys grow up using flyrods as naturally and unself-consciously as we had used cane poles, I was not an absolute disgrace as a flycaster, although I had to correct a sidearmed tendency, that came from all those days of trying to put a bass bug back up under tree limbs, close in against the base of a cypress.

Once in a while, a good cast would bring a fish, and even a small fish on the flyrod was worth two or three taken by any other means. Daddy understood my delusions; when the bright little redbreast or sombre bream was in the boat, he might commend him: "Nice how he hit that bug." Then, lapsing into an exaggerated country accent, "Lak one of them rainbow trout, on a ri-yal coachman." This affectation of rusticity was a kind of counterpoise, a reminder that we were, after all, fishing for panfish and the occasional small bass here on the Waccamaw River, where even using the flyrod at all involved a quixotic pretense, one that would have looked equally ridiculous to a real trout fisherman and to any local river rat who happened to paddle around the corner and see us there.

And yet that pretense was more widely and deeply established than you might imagine. All through Daddy's boyhood and still in mine, among countrypeople and townspeople alike, the universal name for largemouth bass, the sportiest fish in the river, was "trout." This was not because these people had read *Sports Afield* or anything else, but was no doubt because their antecedents from England and Scotland, arriving in a strange and ill-defined country, felt a need to have some fish they could know by this exalted title, and the bass, although in no way resembling a trout, was the worthiest candidate. It was the same instinct that led them to name the muddy little hamlet, which eventually became Conway, by its original name of Kingston—a nostalgia for royalty.

A good deal of water has passed under the bridge. Now when I read "Big Two-Hearted River," I am conscious of how hard Nick must work to make every detail of his trip into a sacrament. There is a right way to catch grasshoppers and a right way to release small trout. And Nick is disproportionately vexed because he cannot remember how to make coffee—was it he or Hopkins who had maintained that it should be boiled, should not be boiled? It is important that he remember! In other stories, Nick is always telling himself how one day he will write it all down, and we have the unpleasant sense of Nick Adams, and, behind him, of Ernest Hemingway too, as being the ego-imprisoned tourists of their own experience, obliged to tell themselves self-ratifying stories about what they are doing as they do it. But in "Big Two-Hearted River," you can almost feel Nick's effort to suppress his self-important interior monologues. Insofar as he can—insofar as anybody can— he pulls the curtain between himself and that invisible gallery of spectators to whom we all play: parents, lovers, rivals, critics, the people we emulate and the ones we detest, but whose unsympathetic eyes we still feel upon us, driving us to self-justification.

Nick isn't completely successful; perhaps nobody is. The mind goes on, running out ahead of experience, lagging behind it, watching itself watching itself. Nick's idyll has a self-consciousness about it; it would not be convincing otherwise. I think my favorite moment in the story comes when he has established his camp ("He was in his home where he had made it") and cooked his supper of canned beans and spaghetti, waited hungrily for it to cool enough not to blister his tongue; then, apprehensively, trying to make the exact compromise between the sensitivity of his tongue and the urgency of his hunger, he takes the first bite—not a cautious, exploratory nibble, but a full spoonful. " 'Chrise,' Nick said, 'Geezus Chrise,' he said happily." You know that his pleasure is in the simple fact of the food, but also in the sound of his own voice, speaking in the idiom of his boyhood. He has had a long walk and a long wait but he is now back into the sanctuary or happy valley that childhood retroactively becomes, once you have escaped from it. There he is, having made it to manhood, watching and hearing himself being a boy.

Daddy persisted in taking me fishing, although I am sure, from my knowledge both of him and of myself, that there would have been many times when he might have preferred to fish alone. The great days that you have on the river always come when you are alone. I do not know why this is so, but it is so. Yet Daddy kept putting up with the inconvenient and incompetent companionship of an actual boy, in place of the idealized boy of his own memory, and thus forgoing a good deal of the intensely private and almost self-sufficing happiness of fishing. In its place there emerged something else, the selfish happiness that the paddler and the fisherman learned to take in each other's skill and success. It took me longer than it might have taken another boy to develop the skill, and that was frustrating; and the success was never more than intermittent, but that was simply fishing, the way fishing is. Reliable success would kill it.

Just after Nick finishes his supper and drinks the coffee, remembering Hopkins, he feels his mind starting to work. Hopkins belongs to the outside world, to the past. We don't know much about him, and it doesn't matter. All that matters is that, for a moment, Hopkins serves to remind Nick of things that need thinking about. But, Hemingway tells us, Nick is tired enough that he can choke thought off, keep it at bay. He will sleep well. But we have been reminded—and his story is so persuasive that we *need* to be reminded—that Nick's experience is an artificial experience, one carefully sealed off, in the way that a tennis match or a chess game is sealed off, from the ruck and confusion of ordinary life. I will now say one more thing about this story, and then get on with my own: the fishing trip, the tennis match, the game of chess seal off the outside world, but they also become, for the participant, highly stylized, abstract representations of that world, with its possibilities of success and failure, its inherent difficulties and its opportunities that unpredictably open for an instant. When the big fish runs all the line off the reel, jumps once, and breaks the leader, Nick sits down, sick and shaken. And he refuses to fish in the cedar swamp, although he knows good fish will be there. The Big Two-Hearted River is a sanctuary; we are told that when Nick had made his camp, nothing could touch him: "He was there, in the good place." But, upon our entry into them, sanctuaries become microcosms. We carry the excluded world in our memories and even in our daydreams, and it can suddenly surface in the form of a big mudfish or of the dark cedar swamp into which the Big Two-Hearted River disappears. Nick knows better than to go there: "in the fast deep water, in the half light, the fishing would be tragic. In the swamp fishing was a tragic adventure. Nick did not want it." But at the end of his story, he is still thinking about it, tempted.

By the time I was through with my first year of college, I knew that I would not return to Conway again, except as a visitor. It was not a decision; it involved no weighing and balancing of considerations, nor any clear sense of what the alternatives might be. Moving away and living elsewhere were simply going to be part of my education, as college itself would be; only this education could have no official conclusion. Sons of course need to get away, inwardly if not outwardly, from fathers, and that need may be more rather than less if there are deep compatibilities between them. None of this was very plain to me; all that was plain was that my homesickness, which was often acute, was not alleviated when I went home for vacation. It was as though *Conway* were not a place but a stage of ontogenic development that somebody, without consulting me, had now declared to be finished, if not completed.

I worked or travelled in the summers; Daddy and I fished when there was opportunity, but there weren't many opportunities. It did not change—still the upper Waccamaw, one man fishing while the other paddled. In this matter, we understood each other and did not need to discuss anything. The paddler knew where the boat should be for the next cast; the fisherman knew where the cast was supposed to go, and put it there. It would be hard to say how far this tacit understanding extended beyond fishing. We avoided more general discussions in part, I think, because we got along so well without them, and felt that they would get mired in all the secondary issues on which we were sure to disagree—politics, opinions, tastes. I am not sure what the primary issues were—the deeper convergings and divergings of our own natures, I suppose. And I think we avoided discussions because we knew that they wouldn't do much good. I had been deeply influenced by him, and the influence may have become in some ways reciprocal; but it was not going to be clarified or changed through anything spoken. My life would not be here, and it would not be in the mold of his life. We fished the river late one summer, just before I was to go off to graduate school; he cast the plug in toward a creek mouth while I held the boat back in the current, and, not speaking directly to me but as though to himself, paid me a compliment which I still remember: "Damn. Higher education is sho' depriving me of a good paddler."

You don't forget about fishing. You never look at a body of water—ocean, lake, or even a greasy river sliding along the quays and docks of a city waterfront—without a speculative and appraising interest. For four years the water I saw was mostly the Charles River, from the Cambridge side. It could be beautiful at night, black and still as pitch against the glitter of Boston, and the first fine days of spring would bring out sailboats, erratic, dipping and veering like kites in a spanking breeze. But the Charles did not reward closer examination. I saw a good many rats swimming in it for what appeared to be purely recreational purposes, and a few incongruously elegant night herons; but, although Boston and Cambridge during those years were full of visionaries, mythomaniacs, neo-pastoralists, Emersonians, men and women blessed with what seemed to me every variety of hope, obsession, and delusion imaginable, and although most of these, at one time or another, would gravitate toward the Charles, drawn to water in the way that people are, I never saw a single soul fishing there. If the cane pole, cork, and cricket, and the bream and redbreast of the Waccamaw had suggested one sort of limited and unglamorous destiny to me, this viscid and fishless river suggested another. This one seemed a destiny I had chosen, advancing to meet the looming American future instead of waiting for it to come and get me.

I knew from what I read that the days of the Big Two-Hearted River were over, and that most trout fishermen would be happy to have the small one that Nick so carefully releases. The story could be read again and again; it could be understood, as all intensely felt fiction can be understood, in ways that are not transient, although the circumstances that produce it are. But the literal fact was that even big-time sportsmen with money to burn, able to fly to Labrador or Alaska and catch trout and salmon of epic dimensions, would find the proportions of Nick's trip, its inward harmony of simplicity and complexity, echoing and re-echoing the experience of the boy and the man, beyond their means. It appeared that my life might have been prefigured by those hot summer afternoons when I lay low in the face of meagre possibilities, and read about places that I could never truly experience, a history and a country that I had not possessed in time.

I married, moved to Maine, began teaching, began a family. And, as soon as I had lived in the state for the six months necessary to establish an official residency, bought a fishing license. Maine had been a famous and fabulous place from the sporting magazines, and, like all such places, it had no more geographical definition in my mind than the land of Canaan or the land of Cockaigne. I didn't know where to begin, so, since both instinct and convenience suggested it, I began near home. I bought local topographical maps and studied them like a prospector, feeling sure that, by walking and beating the bushes, I could find trout streams nobody bothered with, places where I could stake a claim and establish myself as an overnight native. Those early years were busier than any years have ever been, before or since, but I still managed to investigate every rill, brook, bog, and river within twenty miles. In one or two I caught fingerling trout; I would have caught more if I had fished closer to the road, where the hatchery truck dumped them in. In most I found, after toiling and sweating through the astonishingly rank undergrowth of a New England summer, nothing but frogs, tadpoles, crawfish, and mosquitoes.

There was other fishing. I had a canoe, and on local lakes and rivers, fishing in exactly the way I knew how to fish, I caught largemouth bass, pickerel, and panfish. Except that you might come upon a moose instead of an alligator, it all seemed utterly familiar, and, if anything, easier and more productive than in the Waccamaw. I had fine mornings on quiet little rivers that wound through a country of ragged pastures and alder bogs, and sometimes caught fish in sizes and quantities that would have been worth bragging about in Conway. But here they might as well have been mudfish—that was the prevailing local view, and I came to share it. The bass in particular, even some pretty big ones, were torpid and half-hearted, and their flesh was soft and tasted weedy.

There were rumors of trout, rumors of landlocked salmon. A sure sign of the provincial intelligence is an aversion to asking questions—you feel that you ought to know things instinctively, as though you had been born to them, because that is precisely how you do know what you know best. But I finally yielded, talked to a few people, and one day found myself driving north, upriver. I went through towns that had grown up around dam sites, past big, gaunt mills that had spun Carolina cotton in their day, and through the gone-to-seed dairy country of central Maine. Then these poor farms got poorer, the grass sparser, and the country higher. Finally agriculture played out altogether, and the only towns were nothing more than a few stores and shops on either side of the highway, with compact neighborhoods of tin-roofed houses clustered around a pulp mill or saw mill. The river valley, now flanked by steep wooded ridges, narrowed. Driving, losing the river, regaining sight of it a few miles further upstream, a few feet more above sea-level, was like looking through a lens that was being progressively adjusted, brought to clearer focus and higher resolution, until finally what I was looking at was what anybody on God's green earth who had ever dreamed even the most rudimentary dream of fishing would recognize as a trout river.

At the last upstream bridge, just before the river entered a gorge and the highway angled away from it, striking out cross-country toward Quebec, I stopped and walked down to the water. It was late morning on a bright June day, and it was twenty years ago, but what I still remember is the dewy coolness in the shadow of the abutments, the barn swallows nesting on the girders, and the look of that water, funnelling into a long pool above the bridge.

In a Small Pond

It was green and clear, and there was something strange about it, which comes back to me every time I return. Heraclitus would prepare you for the fact that, no matter how often you have seen a river before, every time you see it is the first time, because the river you saw has flowed away, and the one you see is flowing away, and so are you. But this was reverse Heraclitus: as though, setting eyes on the river for the first time, I had already seen it many times before, both in its freshness and familiarity. Once or twice, I have had an analogous sensation in meeting people, knowing that they would matter and last in my life, because they seemed to come out of some part of it that I had forgotten or given up on, and that had managed to stay alive without my noticing.

The first few times Daddy and I went up to try the river, we stayed at the Maxwell Hotel: actually, in a housekeeping cabin across the highway from the hotel. The cabin was cheap and, when you sat on the back porch, you looked twenty feet straight down into the river. Otherwise, there was nothing to recommend it, and that, in an odd way, recommended it to us both. The Maxwell had once catered to a fancier class of sportsman; there was a dining room, a small bar, and even a pool table in the hotel proper, and on the walls were mounted brook trout and landlocked salmon of a size that would have sent a shiver down the spine of Nick Adams. Beneath each fish a small brass plaque gave vital and mortal statistics: weight, length, where and how caught, and the name of the fisherman and where he came from. By now, those fishermen are as dead as the fish: fish, fishermen, and the Maxwell Hotel seemed to have flourished c. 1900–29, and, by the early 1970's, the hotel itself had gone a long way toward joining its clients and their conquests in dusty oblivion.

The proprietor, Martin Lemay, lived in the hotel with his wife and four children, who peeked out from behind doors or beneath the pool table whenever a customer walked in, the older ones giggling and intrigued, the younger ones timid. They responded to all questions in English by gazing mutely at you for a minute, then calling out in lilting voices, their eyes never leaving yours: *Mamá! Papá!* Depending on whether the footsteps you heard coming through the kitchen or down the stairs were light or heavy, they would then say "Elle vient" or "Il vient," duck their heads, and scuttle away, like a child leaving the stage after its first recital. As far as we could tell, Martin Lemay's entire vocation consisted of occasionally renting one of the four cabins that overhung the river. He kept up the grounds, mowing the grass at almost a dead run, sometimes with his youngest son bouncing on his shoulders. He was a stocky, quick, and active man, with an air of having pressing business elsewhere; he would drum his fingers and fidget while we signed the guest book or settled the bill.

But whatever it was that occupied or preoccupied him, it wasn't hotel management. The screens in the cabins were rotten, which, as Daddy pointed out, would have been a real drawback if the windows had opened. The furnishings and appliances were mismatched and obviously scavenged: a couple of swaybacked metal cots, chairs whose cane bottoms, long since collapsed, had been replaced by plywood, a stove that didn't work at all, an electric frying pan that did, and a hot plate that generated more heat at the plug than in the coil. Only a big enamelled iron bathtub, sitting up on four clawed feet, and a gas hot water heater that looked like some nefarious apparatus from Frankenstein's laboratory, but was probably state of the art in 1920, suggested the comparative luxury of these quarters forty or fifty years ago, when prosperous Yankees from Boston and the North Shore had come up for a taste of the Maine woods, and a chance at the big jut-jawed fish that hung, glassy-eyed and darkened with age, on the dining room walls.

Daddy and I improvised, made our morning coffee by boiling water in the electric frying pan, put up with mice and mosquitoes. It was a small price to pay for not having to feel like sports, pam-

pered and catered to and insulated. We fished the river and found
it hard going, and that, too, was somehow a recommendation.
You are not to imagine that we were high-minded, catch-and-
release, art-for-art's-sake fishermen. We wanted to catch fish and
bring them home, cook 'em and eat 'em, but we accepted, and
perhaps even welcomed, the frustrations. Analogies between fishing and religion, love, inspiration, and the other great inconclu-
sive cravings ought always to be made with an absolutely
unmistakable wry and rueful irony; but get down under the skin
of any real fisherman, past all talk of tippets and leaders and patterns and hatches, shooting heads and weighted nymphs, and you
find a man who is still and always fishing for something that he
can only know through the lifelong experience of not catching it.
He seeks to progressively rarefy the quality of his failure. There
was a kind of consolation for us in knowing that we were in no
danger of exhausting the fascination of what was difficult; we could
only hope it would not exhaust us.

We caught small fish, immature salmon and little trout. These
eight- and ten-inchers implied larger ones, but, during those first
years of our apprenticeship, we not only never caught anything
bigger, we never even saw any evidence that such a thing existed—
no hair-raising heavy swirling rise beside a rock, no mighty strike,
just when you least expected it, to break the leader. With me,
anyway, perhaps the problem was that there was no time when I
least expected it. I would begin a story with every cast, watching
the fly drift, waiting on the fish to supply the punch line. He
never did; I would cast again, begin the story again.

Each trip, when we walked over to the hotel to settle up, Martin Lemay would ask how the fishing had been, and one or the
other of us would deflect the question by answering in the time-
honored way—"Nothing special," or "A few small ones"—hoping
that this might be construed as understatement. But Martin was
pretty literal-minded. "Where you fish?" he'd say, and we'd say
mostly in the river. "She's been slow this year," he'd say. "I fish

her a little tis morning, right t'er behind ta cabin. Only catch two fish. Salmon, two-t'ree pound apiece. But, cheeze, I lose a good one." He never showed us the fish, these two- and three-pound salmon, and, driving back down toward Bowdoinham, we could never decide whether we would rather know if he was telling the truth, or not know it.

There were the big fish on the walls of the hotel, and the hotel itself, to evoke the heroic age of the North Woods, and, along the river, when the water was down, you would occasionally come across a more potent artifact—the iron point of a peavy or cant-hook, pitted with rust and abraded by water and rock until it looked like something left by a westward-errant Viking, although in fact it dated from well within living memory. A lot of pine timber had floated down this river, and lumberjacks had guided it, scrambling out with their legendary hob-nailed agility to pry or dynamite the jams, and sometimes losing more than a peavy. Martin remembered the last fatality, twenty years ago; "He fall in just about up t'ere around Black Brook Sluice. May, and she'd been runnin' high, right up in ta bushes. Couldn't find 'im, so t'ey close the dam, and bring the river down just as low as in the summer-time. Perfect. I tell you it was two day of beautiful fishin' I had til t'ey find 'im. Like t'ey say, every cloud's got a silver linin' to it somewheres."

Coming to it this late, we more or less assumed that what we found in northern Maine would remain as it was—diminished and diluted from the wilderness it once had been, but not subject to further erosion. The river would be there, and the North Woods, now producing pulp wood instead of saw timber, would go on being a big stretch of impressively empty country, lightly veined with logging roads, some of them active, others halfway back to impassability, and others completely gone—new ones being con-structed, we reckoned, at about the same rate that the old ones reverted to puckerbrush. Every morning—sometimes early, some-times not until almost noon—the gates on an upstream dam that we had never seen would open, and the first we would know of it would be a four-foot bolt of pulpwood, bobbing downstream toward us. We'd scramble to the bank, the water would rise like a very fast tide, and within three or four minutes the river we were fishing would be swallowed by a much bigger and more dangerous-looking river, full of standing waves and pulpwood. The logs tossed and jostled against each other; you could imagine lemmings or caribou or bison. But it was only pulp, bound for the mills downriver. Being in short lengths, it never jammed, and so required no lumberjacks to shepherd it. A lot got caught in backwaters and left on the bank; some sank to the bottom, and that was simply the river's carrying charge, accepted as a cost of doing business. The water would stay up for the rest of the day, and we would need to find a pond or stream for our afternoon fishing. After dark, the gates would close, and the river we were coming to feel proprietary about would return during the night, and be there for us—dark, sleek-pooled, and classic—the following morning. Like the fish and all the lesser life that sustained them—mayfly, caddisfly, sculpin, hellgrammite, midge—we adjusted to the river's schedule as though it were a natural dispensation, perhaps inconvenient but permanent; and we developed certain adaptive behaviors. The chief of these was the habit of looking upstream as regularly and reflexively as a motorist on an interstate checking the rearview mirror. We would be watching for one thing—that first, premonitory piece of pulpwood, the signal to get ashore, quick.

In the mid-seventies, the paper companies and the state reached an agreement to phase out the pulp drives. It was all in the papers: on the one hand, the End of an Era; on the other hand, promises of improvement in the river's water quality and recreational potential. As soon as the agreement was reached, the paper companies set about exponentially expanding their network of roads, since they would henceforth need to rely on trucks to get the logs to the mills, and this, I can now see, marked the beginnings of a transformation. The North Woods were to lose most of their remaining remoteness; ponds and streams and stretches of river that once had been well-kept secrets, accessible only to fishermen who knew the old overgrown roads, and were willing to risk washed-out bridges and beaver-flooded causeways, and to lug a canoe a mile or so for an evening of fishing, became available to just about any greenhorns, Daddy and me included. The last pulp drive was in 1974; and as we drove up the following year for our first trip, we were pleased to think that we would now have for ourselves a river that lasted all day, and no longer ebbed and flowed at the behest of the Scott Paper Company. As always, we felt that this would be the trip that justified all our faith, patience, meekness, and so forth. We didn't want to inherit the earth, just to bring home a few good fish. "I'm not getting any younger," Daddy said, by way of diffident reminder and supplication.

And he almost didn't get much older. We went to the river early next morning and walked upstream from the bridge. We fished what had become our favorite pool—the Elbow, where the river made a sharp dogleg at the foot of a rapid—with no urgency and small success. Below that pool, in the middle of the river, was a gravel bar, separated from the near bank by a quick run, and from the far bank by a narrow, shaded glide of surprisingly deep water. In the previous years, I had occasionally waded out to the bar and fished the far side of it. It was a nervous business, being out there and worrying about the river rising, and the few fish I caught from the gravel bar were no better than usual, but it was a beautiful place to fish, and the risk seemed, in some irrational way, as though it ought to enhance the possibilities. So, late in the morning, when the sunlight had worked its way down the west side of the gorge and driven the shadows from the Elbow Pool, I waded out to the upper end of the gravel bar and began fishing my way down it. I had to remind myself not to worry. The day was turning warm, but the water on the far side of the run lay

in deep shadow, and still had the look and promise of early morning on it. I had caught two nine-inch trout by the time I reached
the end of the bar; in those days, that constituted real success.
The second one took the dry fly just at the tail end of the bar,
where the river rejoined itself, and after I netted him, I looked
upstream, and saw that Daddy had followed me, and was now at
the upper end of the bar.

He was fishing intently. As I watched, he cranked in and changed
flies, something he seldom did. He cast no more than half a dozen
times with the new fly to a spot close in under the dark ledges of
the far bank, then cranked in and changed again. I turned back to
my own business, killed the trout, tied on a fresh fly, and took
one more glance back upriver. Daddy had obviously spotted
something, and I hoped I might see him standing there with the
rod bowed and a big fish on. Instead what I saw was the river
upstream. In the quiet sunlit stillness, the Elbow Pool was disappearing, a stationary surf standing in it. I yelled; Daddy looked
up, and saw me pointing, and I watched him turn, see the river
coming, and start toward shore.

It was all very deliberate; he had a staff, and had to move carefully on the slick rocks. It was like watching a dog start out across
a busy expressway, and seeing that he isn't going to make it. He
got across the gravel bar and into the run between it and the
shore, and then I could see the river starting to rise around him.
At first it simply looked like every step was taking him into slightly
deeper water; but the depth wasn't the problem. The problem was
the weight of the current. He was bearing down heavily on his
staff, planting it upstream of himself, trying to keep in contact
with the bottom. Waist deep and still twenty feet from shore, he
lost his feet. He threw away the staff and tried to swim, holding
the rod aloft in one hand, but the river had him now. He threw
the rod away too, and I positioned myself directly downstream,
hoping I might be able to grab him when he came by. But it wasn't

necessary. He thrashed on into shallow water, and not even trying to stand up, hauled himself out onto the bank like a seal. The water was just reaching me as I waded ashore.

When I got up to him he was still sitting on the bank. He had the gray-faced, shrunken look that people have when coming out of shock or surgery. I asked him if he was all right. I wasn't sure he heard. He slowly set about unfastening the harness on his waders and unbuckling his belt, and his hands shook. I took the waders by the ankles and pulled them off, held them up, and dumped them. There was a ton of water in them, and the fear that postpones itself in an emergency settled onto me. We were under cedars—the air sweet with that cedar-chest smell you associate with blankets and mothballs, the snug securities of domestic life— and I moved into a patch of sunlight and hunkered there, baseball-catcherwise. The sun on the back of my shirt was an animal consolation, and the river—how to put it?—the river had gone from being something sudden and terrible, like an avalanche, back into just being a river again, inconveniently high for fishing, but still and all nothing more than a bright, bold river, beautiful in its energy.

Daddy leaned forward and pulled off his socks. He squeezed the water out of them and put them back on carefully, as though he were dressing for a ceremonial occasion. Then he looked at me and finally spoke: "I see no particular necessity for your mother's hearing about this." And he grinned a wan grin.

I gestured toward where the gravel bar had been. "What was over there?"

"Salmon. He rose just after you left. I got him to roll once at the fly. His back bowed right up out of the water."

"How big?"

"Big."

"But *how* big?"

He held his hands apart. Big.

In a Small Pond

That night, in the still room, Daddy's breathing was at first the only noise I could hear. Breathing sounds least assured in the early stages of sleep; there would be the second's hesitation between exhaling and inhaling, as though something in him were mustering the will to draw the next breath, and when he let that breath go it passed out of him with a kind of shudder. He had never talked much about mortality, beyond an occasional matter-of-fact reference to threescore and ten, the biblical allotment that he was approaching with no sign of panic or protest. His sense of limits and proportions, a practical objectivity that I took for granted until I discovered how rare it was, had always sustained him; he did not ask that God, fate, or biology exempt him. Or that was how it had always seemed to me. But today had been different—that suddenness, the struggle to swim with waders filling with water, holding him back, and the humiliating awareness of our folly, our lack of sensible precaution. We hadn't said much in the long, rough walk from the Elbow Pool down to the bridge, and when we got back, I left him fussing with the bacon in the electric frying pan, and went over to speak to Martin. "Oh she come up same as always," he said. "T'ats a power station upstream. T'ey get the call from Boston or wherever, t'ey open her up. She'll come up early one day, late the next. You got to look out. Same as always." When I relayed this information to Daddy, he said he believed that he could have figured it out for himself: the evidence, although circumstantial, had been overwhelming.

We would fish the river again—same as always—on the next trip up. But not again on this trip. That was what I thought as I lay in the cot. It wasn't a tragic adventure we'd had—even the rod he'd lost wasn't his best one. It was a serious and salutary scare, and we had gotten off lightly. I thought about the men with whom he had fished and hunted while I was growing up, and how timid and unenterprising they had grown with age, as though they had come to see only risk and hazard in anything that fell outside their own dwindling, fussy routines, or lay beyond the doorstep. It was something like hypochondria, and Daddy had no use for it. But when he and I had poured our whiskey before supper and I had started out to the porch, where we customarily sat and drank and watched the river, he said something about its being chilly—why didn't we just sit in the kitchen where the light was better anyway? And so we had.

Tomorrow morning I would propose that we do what we had sometimes talked about doing—pack a lunch, leave early, and make a day of it on Big David Pond. And that was what I did and that was what we did. But in the meantime I slept erratically, finally dozed off about midnight and woke an hour or so later. Daddy's breathing was quieter. Listening in the other direction, I could now tell that the river was back down to its morning level. When it was up, it sounded like a heavy wind in the trees, only steadier and bigger. If you let yourself listen to it too much at night, you would begin to metabolize it, and feel the pressure of dementia, of a noise you couldn't keep out. And then the pressure would ease, so gradually you wouldn't recognize it. The river didn't drop all at once; it relented slowly, smoothing out and abating until at last it whispered and murmured conversationally, and you could eavesdrop if you wanted to or do as I finally did, tune it out and go to sleep.

We reached Little David Pond before mid-morning, and I carried the canoe down, while Daddy brought everything else—rods, paddles, and a pack basket with tackle, lunch, and even a camera. This was deluxe fishing, a family outing. It was a short paddle across Little David to the portage, and then a carry of something less than a quarter of a mile into Big David. Seen from underneath a canoe, the trail is nasty, buggy, rocky, and astonishingly elastic, stretching itself out, withholding your destination. But finally you see the glitter of water through the dark spruce trunks ahead, step out into sunlight and onto a big slab of granite that slopes off into the pond, duck yourself out from under the canoe with a flip and a twist, cradle it against your thighs, and slide it into the water. Done. It sits there, all lightness and buoyancy now, in its natural habitat, and you can just about levitate with your sudden weight-lessness.

Big David sits in a shallow bowl of hills; it is roughly circular and about a half a mile across. It is enclosed, removed, and cleanly defined, like a garden, and that is what I like and don't like about it, and about ponds in general—the sense of being sequestered from disruptive possibilities, set down in a world of small and perfect proportions. We had first fished Big David the previous summer, and had caught fish. The trout here were chunkier and more vivid than in the river, and they tended to be ten or eleven inches long, instead of eight or nine. What was missing was not actuality, and perhaps not even potentiality, but only the right setting for a certain kind of dream—the fish that lurks in the deep pool at the foot of the rapid, probably a salmon, landlocked now but still containing within himself the power and the wild, free life of the river, its old connectedness to oceanic immensities. I had thought about that earlier in the morning, when we had left the cabin and driven across the bridge, and I had looked upstream and seen the long pool, misty and heavily shadowed, and the water coming down out of the gorge into it. I had felt a petulant disappointment in leaving it behind, as though today's trip were our last, as though there might never be another chance at the river. I recognized the childishness of the feeling, and rebuked myself for it; that did no good whatsoever.

But at least the portage was over; the canoe was ready and waiting, and we were going to go fishing. We took the rods out of their cases and rigged them. As we had driven in the last stretch of woods road—unimproved, more like a streambed than a road, but still passable—we had noticed, hovering around every size-able mudpuddle, the small electric blue dragonflies that are locally called darning needles. Their official name, mysteriously, is dam-selfly. They were more in evidence when we crossed Little David, and now, as we paddled out into Big David, they were all around, like bees in clover. Fish were rising, intercepting them in their transition from aquatic to aerial existence; occasionally a small trout would fling itself into the air, like a soccer goalie making a save, and nab one on the wing. In the middle of the pond a single rock the size of a refrigerator juts up, and the damselflies were around it like seabirds around a rookery—some perched on the rock, having just shed their skins and completed their astonishing metamorphosis; others pausing and darting, clasping and coupling in air. Daddy cast to the rock and immediately caught a fine eleven-incher.

Pond fish are notoriously manic-depressive. They will feed exuberantly for half an hour and then stop, and the pond, that had a moment before been all life and animation, simply goes dead, as though somebody had thrown a switch. Today we had the whole pond to ourselves, and I could not believe that what we had come upon would last. Wherever we looked there were the spreading rings left by rising fish. Those in range did not always take the fly that was cast to them, but they did not always refuse it, and that is all you ask: the tense watching, the possibility of failure to give meaning to success. None of the fish was bigger than the first one Daddy had caught, but several were nearly as big. When my eyes tired of staring into the glazed refraction of the water, I could lift them to the shoreline, and follow the rise of the land—tier upon tier of hemlock, spruce, fir, birch, and pine—up to the top of the ridge, and watch the low clouds passing behind a big, twisted pine that stood out against the sky. The canoe rocked gently, and it would look as though the pine itself, and the whole ridge, were moving stealthily, counterclockwise around the pond; as though the clouds beyond were what was stationary.

A splashy strike would bring me back—damn! missed! And just in front of my face there would be a damselfly wavering in thin air, then darting off at such speed that the air seemed to have swallowed it; then appearing again, Tinkerbelle redivivus. More prosaic ones settled on the rod tip or on the line; sometimes one would take an amorous interest in the fly as it sat on the water, and hover and buzz around it with such excitement that we could hear the tiny crackling of its wings, like cellophane uncrumpling. When the sun caught their wings they sparkled and glinted and looked like light slowed down, so that you could glimpse it as something that the air was full of.

Around noon, the weather thickened, and the next time I looked at the ridgeline veils of rain were there, and we watched them come down to us. That would be the end of the fishing, I thought, and then we were sitting in something more than a mist and less than a drizzle, and the pond was quiet. We had six fish, had missed many more, and were content. We ate our lunch, and before we had finished the intermission was over, the sun was back, and it all started again. And that was how the afternoon went—we would fish in calm bright sunshine, and then see another cloud blow in across the hills, sit as the mist descended toward us, reached and shrouded us, then passed on. Once, in midafternoon, the sky went almost black and a sharp hard rain hissed across the pond. The big drops pocked and silvered the surface of the water until, Daddy said, it looked like a cheese grater. But that too went away, a powerful premonition of something that didn't happen. The singing of birds resumed, the damselflies and trout picked up where they had left off, and we kept catching fish.

Only in retrospect do that alternation of weathers and splurge of wild trout seem dream-like. Hunting or fishing involves being in the wrong place at the wrong time, or the right place at the wrong time, or the wrong place at the right time much more commonly than people imagine; the variables are complex, mysterious, and like all occult things, they seem to include among themselves the mood and faith of the seeker, as well as the properties of the thing sought. But being in the right place at the right time does not therefore feel like an extraordinary benefaction. It simply feels right, the way good weather and good health do. You have the sense of having arrived at a conclusion that, once you have reached it, seems self-evident.

The limit in those days was eight fish per fisherman. We had had six at lunch, and tried to keep mental count of them after that. As we caught them, we put them in a live basket. When we pulled it out of the water to add another one, there was no possibility of checking the tally, with the fish all writhing and squirming together in the bottom of the basket. By about six o'clock, a heavier drizzle had settled over the pond, and we reckoned that we had fifteen fish. This once, it seemed important that we should catch the limit, fill out the day. We let the canoe drift over to the big rock, hoping there might be something special for a finale, but instead, at the same time, each of us hooked a fish of average size. We got them both in, saw that there was nothing to choose between them, and so I threw mine back, as it was the less deeply hooked.

Daddy suggested that we gut the fish there in the canoe, anchored by the rock, rather than on shore, where it would be buggy. Being methodical and tidy, he dismantled his rod, took off the reel, and slid the rod into its case and the reel into his pocket before taking out his knife. I took two fish from the basket, one for him and one for me, and we got down to it. Gutting a trout is scarcely messier or more time-consuming than peeling an orange: a sharp crack with the knife handle to break the neck, then notching out the vent, slitting the belly, stripping the cavity clean. We each used a paddle, laid across the gunwales, for a worktable. After we had flung the guts of the first trout into the water, a seagull came over to watch; within five minutes he was joined by four others, that materialized out of the air as quietly and inevitably as the drizzle had. They fought and squabbled over the guts that floated on the surface, tried clumsily to seize them out of the air. We were to them what the damselflies had been to the trout and the trout had been to us—an upwardly mobile part of the food chain. The trout had had their moment of natural bonanza and we had

had ours, and now our moment had passed, and the excitement had gone out of our day. We kept our heads down, and, with the drizzle and the cold beginning to sink in, felt a weariness and faint oppression of the spirits that were making a perfect prelude for the solemn and measured whiskey we would each have while we cooked supper, back at the cabin. There was still the ugly lug of the canoe across the portage, and the long, rough drive out. And still two more fish to go, one for him and one for me. Fourteen were laid out neatly on the floor of the canoe. I reached into the basket and there was one fish.

"Well," I said, and "Well," he said. It wasn't a complete sur-prise—our scorekeeping had been belated and haphazard. No reason not to stop with fifteen; that was already an indecent abun-dance of trout. But the law authorized one more. "Shouldn't have thrown that other one back," Daddy said. "Take your rod and catch him again." I told him to use my rod while I cleaned the fifteenth fish, but he wouldn't, and so I started casting. Daddy cleaned the fish. Nothing bit. The fly was sodden and scarcely floated, but I didn't feel like changing it. I was ready for the cabin and the end of the day, food and drink and dry clothes.

Not many fish were feeding now. You would look for a long time at the pearly surface of the pond and see it unblemished by any dimple. But the occasional rises, most of them far out, now looked bigger, in an indefinable way—the swirls were slower and quieter and somehow weighty. "Look," I said to him, "if we're going to catch this fish, you better put your rod back together and get to work." Finally he relented, began fumbling in his pocket for his reel, and explaining as he did so that it looked like the only way I was going to catch that last fish was for him to go through the whole procedure, reassemble his rod, put the reel back on, draw the line out through the guides, pick out a fly, tie it on, and then, he said, just as he was all set to cast, I would catch a fish and he would have to take the whole damn thing apart again.

"Fine," I said. "Hurry up with it." So he screwed the reel back down to its seat, joined the two sections of the rod together, and began threading the line through the guides. This is an awkward procedure in a canoe, and I leaned forward to hold the butt of the rod for him, so that he could thread the tip. He looked at me, holding his rod inattentively in one hand, while holding my own with the other, and trying to keep my eyes on the fly out in the water, forty or fifty feet away. He told me not to worry; the fish wouldn't bite until it had made him finish the last step of assembling his tackle, and he had gotten his fly tied on. That was a laborious job for him, with his farsighted eyes and fingers that had gotten a little stiff and unwieldy in the cool wet air. He held the fly out far from his face, and, with a certain amount of exasperated grunting, got the leader through the eye of the hook and coiled back around itself in the standard fisherman's knot. He took the fly by the hook between his thumb and forefinger and gave it a soft tug to be sure that it was tight, and then, with the air of having finished a prologue to something, he made himself comfortable on the seat of the canoe, looked out to where my fly was floating on the surface, and said, "OK. Brace yourself. He'll bite now."

So, playing out a little comedy, we both sat there for a couple of seconds, I with the rod in a position of exaggerated readiness, he as though breathless with anticipation, and both of us looking intently at a very bedraggled royal coachman, where it lay in the lee of the rock. Daddy was about to say something about the fish having missed its cue, or I was about to say something about his going ahead and casting now, so we could get it over with. Whatever it was never got said. It wasn't the usual quick splashy rise of a small fish, or the slow heavy swirl that might mean a larger one. It was harder to swallow than that. The fish came directly up from under the fly and rose straight up out of the water like a large-mouth bass or a Polaris missile, and then fell back in. It happened so fast, and was so out of proportion to the expectations that we had permitted ourselves to have, that I wanted to point where the fish had been, which was where we had both been looking with undivided attention, and say *"Did you see that?"*

In a Small Pond

❧

I had tightened the line out of a reflex akin to the one that makes you blink your eyes when somebody shoves a hand close to your face. In any case, the fly was gone and there was a heavy, deliberate weight at the end of the line. I played the fish gingerly, not trying to bring him toward the boat. We told each other calmly, like two men discussing the weather, that if he was firmly hooked and you didn't rush him and get him too close too quick, there wasn't much a fish could do in a pond, where there was no current to help him and no snags or branches to flee into. If he wasn't firmly hooked, we explained to each other, there wasn't much the fisherman could do about it. So there was nothing to worry about either way, at least not until time came to try to get him up to the boat and into the net. If you do that too soon, and the fish has more energy left than you reckoned on, he can swirl in panic away from the boat, while the line is tight and short, and tear out the hook or break the leader. Or you get overeager with the net, swipe at him and he swerves, and the net hits the taut line and pop! there goes your fish.

So Daddy kept telling me to take my time about it and I did, and furthermore I had been for some time now. The fish did not jump again or even swim very fast; it felt like he was simply cruising back and forth, sulky about having a fly in his jaw. "Like walking a dog," Daddy said. "Don't rush him." But the fish had a way of occasionally turning toward the boat, so that the line would go slack for an instant, and something—my heart or my lunch— would come right up behind my teeth and I would clamp them shut as I tightened the empty line, and there he would be again, stubborn and sullen and invisible.

I would try to net him myself. If he got away in the last scene of the last act, I wanted to have only myself to blame for it. When he seemed tired—had it been five minutes or twenty since he struck?—I began moving him in toward me, taking in line until it was short enough for me to raise the rod and slide him across the surface toward the net. As he came, we could see the fly, barely caught in his upper lip. I got him almost over the net, looked into his watery eye, and he made a mighty commotion. Not ready yet. I wasn't going to rush him. You rush them you lose them, we explained to each other. He bored down deep, more urgent now but feeling slightly fluttery on the end of the line, as though he were gasping.

But we had both seen, when he had been on the surface near the net, that he was longer than the net was wide. Daddy said for me to give him the net and I did, and then it was time to try again. I angled the rod tip up and toward his end of the canoe, and lifted carefully again, the way you would lift a platform with something fragile on it by a long rope. He came sliding across the surface again, and this time, while he was still too far from the canoe, Daddy suddenly leaned out and swiped the net up under him hard, the way you are never supposed to do it, and before I even had time to curse there was the net up in the air, the fish lying more across it than in it, and then he flopped off, thud, not splash, because Daddy had gotten him over the canoe before he flopped. He lay on the floor between us, the fly still firm in his lip. Daddy had the net in his hand, and had to do something with it. So he laid it carefully over the fish and then put his foot on the handle, as though there were a likelihood of the fish's proving to be something out of a dream, and suddenly getting up off the floor, crawling over the gunwale, and jumping back into the pond. It was a funny gesture, about half-way to being a serious one.

But what we had was really and simply a fish, a good one. I leaned down and unhooked it, broke its neck and laid it out beside the other fish on the floor of the canoe. The quotient of human happiness is easily arrived at—you divide what you have by what you had expected. Sixteen inches long he was; he would turn out to weigh something less than two pounds. Put beside the other trout we had caught that day or any other day, he was elephantine, massive and thick-bodied and out of proportion. Daddy studied him carefully. "Look lak a durned mudfish, if you ast me," he said.

4 A Pastoral Occasion

We at last decided to make an end to things, and put Jacob down. You put an old dog down to abbreviate his suffering, or free yourself of his inconvenience.

He is thirteen, his birthday falling within a month of Elizabeth's. He can scarcely rise unassisted—each morning he looks like a man trying to pull an overturned wagon. Nothing wrong with his forelegs—he is a massive, deep-chested dog. But the hips, congenitally defective, have grown steadily worse. The atrophied thighs lie awkwardly out to the side as he heaves himself up. Then he pulls ahead, his toenails scrabbling against the floor, until the wasted hindquarters trail out behind him. Now he can slowly curl them beneath him, into something like a sitting posture, from which, panting, tottering, he rises. There is no triumph in it. He looks at us with the hangdog look of apology, supplication, and fear.

Age is a terror. He senses the impatience with which we, busy

people with things to do, wait on each labored ascension, so that
we may let him out in the morning and in the evening. Worse
than his mortification is his humility. He wags his hindquarters as
short-tailed dogs do, writhing in gratitude. It is the hideous smile
of a very old, very infirm man. It proclaims his daily knowledge
that he has outlived nature, and must trust to the uncertainties of
our forbearance. He has lived like this for two years. But we cannot appease age, and he grows slowly weaker. Any least thing
trips him—the threshold of a door, a child's shoe.

He is grizzled, his old muzzle almost white, gone gaunt and
surprisingly soft, like threadbare corduroy. His eyes, milky with
cataracts, are reptilian. Strange wrinkled tumors—benign, Harry
Ahern has told us—sprout from his underside and along one flank,
like misplaced nipples or bloated wood ticks. When Bonnie first
came into the house last year, as a six-week-old weanling puppy,
she would sometimes tug at them. He would growl, and once
snapped hard at her, with a speed and savagery that surprised us
all. Bonnie scampered under the stove, yowling with terror, and
he looked up, whimpering, contrite, thumping his stump of tail
on the floor, acknowledging that he had no right to do it, no right
at all. Please forgive again, please once more.

There is more to it. He stinks. His flatulence has become legendary, his breath an abomination. But the worst is a sourness
connected to no bodily process, that emanates from his coat, from
the whole rickety carcass he has dragged through these last years
of his life. Bathing does little good; the smell overrides even the
pleasant, cleanly fragrance of the soap. The stink of mortality
does not wash out, scrub and scour it as you will. Even our youngest daughter shuns him, out of some instinct deeper than fastidiousness.

But his appetite, the most reliable of a dog's vital indicators, is
undiminished. If anything, it is greater than it was in his prime.
He sees little more than shadows, but knows the routines of the
house completely. He can tell at once if I am angry, although he

cannot tell why, and blames himself, cringing and fawning. He knows by the rhythm of traffic through the kitchen when we are leaving on a trip, and hauls himself under the stove, miserable, waiting to be dragged out and taken to the kennel. Such a dog has no difficulty in knowing when it is suppertime, and he will not be put off or placated. At five o'clock he gets up and dogs me, stands in my way, pushes his snout against my leg, until I get his pan. Then his ears lift up, his old eyes gleam with a muddy lambency, and his breath comes in harsh, hoarse gasps. He is underfoot as we go out to the barn and fill the pan; he has his muzzle in it before it touches the floor. His sides heave as he eats. If Bonnie is dilatory or momentarily distracted from her food, he is in her bowl in an instant. Normally the most obedient of dogs, he cannot be called off, and I must grab him by the scruff and lift his head out of the dish, his jaws still working. It is somehow obscene, too much like the old vision of Death as a skeleton whose hunger is never glutted, or a parody of all the unseemly desires that stay with us, long after we should have satisfied or subdued them. Increase of appetite growing by what it feeds on, ravening the devourer.

We are in late summer, the world green and gracious, the fields new mown and studded with big cylindrical bales like tumuli, and the young swallows, fledged now, gathering by dozens, by scores, and at last by hundreds on the wires, skimming out low over the fields, returning, with their squeaky cries, their sudden restlessness. Crickets sing in the stubble at dusk. Our children are healthy, the youngest never more so. She is full of talk and jokes, proudly displays her own small garden of radishes, which prosper, and flowers, plucked the moment they blossom. But there is also the evening news, which this summer revives images of Hiroshima and the Holocaust, and those images, from which no one, no matter how deep in the country, is free, loom out at us again— the sunken eyes and faces, the piled bodies, arms and legs akimbo, waxy white, soft as wax. Victims of the famine in Ethiopia merge with these, at some level below thought; they too stare out, too numbed to brush away the flies that batten on starvation. My children gaze at children whose bellies are taut and round as the swelled throats of the toads that trill around our doorstep each evening.

Meanwhile, we eat well, fresh healthy things from the garden, occasionally a mackerel or bluefish from the teeming summer sea. But our eldest daughter renounces the eating of flesh and flirts— just to scare herself, she says—with anorexia. Between meals she slips into the pantry and stands there, gorging on crackers or potato chips, pressing them by the handful into her mouth. The dog in our midst is not a figure from an allegory, or, if so, from the allegory that also contains ourselves. To get into the pantry, we must shove his heavy bulk aside, making room for the door to swing open.

Great schools of menhaden, driven by voracious bluefish, have crowded their way upriver. It happens each summer. Soon there are too many fish trying to feed and flee and breathe; too much blood and flesh clouding the water after each new onslaught; too little oxygen. Fish—predators and prey—die by the thousands. It is no cause for alarm, a fisheries biologist announces; indeed, it is a sign of the restored health of the river that it occasionally chokes and gags on its own fecundity this way. For Bonnie, it is a boon. She finds dead fish along the tide-line, and rolls in them ecstatically until her coat gleams with scales and tallowy fish grease. She reeks proudly, and cocks her tail with a new jauntiness. Jacob sniffs and licks her as though she were in heat: a seedy, broken-down roué, paying the homage of his creaking gallantry to a fine-fleshed young woman, perfumed, made-up, and ready for an evening's patrolling and prospecting along the boulevards. Ourselves caricatured in canine drag, the mirror nature holds up to our most unnatural extravagances.

Susan and the girls would go over to Bremen on Wednesday, to spend a week with her parents. She would be joined there by

A Pastoral Occasion

~

her cousin and his family—prodigal Martin, who ten years ago left college and fled New England for the Northwest Territory, and who returned last year, with a wife and two children. His father had died in the interval, and he now assumed, effortlessly and unexpectedly, his father's role within the family—healer, restorer, with a gift for releasing the family's impacted and complex affections. His returns, like his father's, have never been long enough or often enough, and they call for the fatted calf, an undeclared, impromptu Thanksgiving. I would join them on Saturday, but first planned for myself two days of fishing up north, on the Penobscot.

We talked it all out on Tuesday. Jacob would never survive another winter. His joints stiffened and grew more painful each year as the cold began to creep into the house. He was becoming incontinent, and could not reliably contain himself at night. Whatever fond memories we might have of the dog were disappearing fast, consumed by what he had become. This would be the time for it. We would not tell the children beforehand. No need for them to know that the old dog, sleeping as usual, whimpering fretfully in his sleep, would die that afternoon. Let them have only their own happiness to consider on Wednesday morning, with the prospect of the drive over to Bremen, then the swimming in the cold, salty tide pond there, and seeing the cousins and grandparents again. If they knew, they would suddenly try to see him, as you try to see familiar places or people when you are about to leave them for good. Their caresses and expiatory attentions, hugs, pats, tears, would only trouble him. I wished to spare them, and myself, their grief. In proportion to their age, it would be less self-conscious, less corroded by the knowledge that it would quickly pass, that it had not been earned by earnest love, that it was adulterated by that generalized pity which is finally self-pity. Hannah's would be Eden-grief—natural tears easily shed, and soon wiped. Elizabeth would know more, and Coles yet more, of the pretense that infects even our most spontaneous sorrows. Out of sight, out of mind, would prevail in the end, so let the sleeping dog lie this morning in sight but out of mind, as he had lain for so many mornings before.

On Wednesday we ate our breakfast. I kissed them goodbye, and went in for a morning in the office. It was a productive morning; my mind was not on the dog. He impinged on my concentration only as the consciousness of something unpleasant—*what was it? O yes. That*—to be done in the afternoon. At noon, I went home and fixed lunch. He pulled himself up and came over, not to be patted but to sniff me thoroughly. Mostly blind, surrounded by the gibberish of human voices, he takes the world in through his nose. As I sat to eat, he barked his stentorian, concussive bark, demanding to be let out. I let him out. As I sat again, he barked again, demanding to be let in. I let him in. This was repeated twice before I had finished my sandwich. He reminds you of someone looking for something mislaid, growing frantic, passing from one room to the next and back again, not sure, after a while, of where he has or has not searched, even of where he is. Jacob's insistence is maddening when this fit seizes him. If you are slow in responding to his bark, he will paw at the door latch with his great forepaw, gouging the wood with his nails. No door in our house he cannot eventually open, no door unscoured by his foot. Often we hear him at night—the steady rasp, rasp of the paw at the door and at last, by blind chance and mindless persistence, the click of the latch and the creaking open of the door.

It was hot. I napped briefly after lunch, then got back up. He was sound asleep when I went out. I shut Bonnie in her pen, got a shovel, and walked across the stubble, to where the pasture slopes down to the river. In the days when the town, and all New England, were intensively farmed, this slope too had been mown and kept, but that had been many years ago. Now chokecherry, viburnum, sumac, and hawthorne had sprung up, and the remaining bits of pasture grass were disappearing under thistle and goldenrod. At the edge of the swampy border between the slope and the river were posted a few knobby apple trees, clogged with dead wood. Slowly, year by year, they were being taken by the alders that crept up from the swamp. They still bore fruit, sparsely or abundantly according to some rhythm of their own, which seemed largely unrelated to the vagaries of the season. The apples were small and of a palate-withering sourness, but grouse loved them, especially once they were softened by the first lethal frosts of October.

I picked a clearing on the slope, where there would be no roots to contend with, removed the sod, and began to dig. Graves are traditionally long and narrow, but a shovel, by the curvature of its blade, wants to dig a round hole. It had been a dry summer, and the soil—the notorious blue clay of Bowdoinham—grew harder as I dug down. Three feet would do for a dog, I told myself—but a full three feet, an honest three feet. A foot below the surface, the clay assumed a consistency almost like shale; it came up in shards and curled shavings. This slowed the work, but pleased me: the shovel carved out walls as clean and definite as the inner walls of an unglazed pot. The blade clinked and scraped in the still heat of early afternoon. When the circular hole was too deep for me to use my foot against the shoulder of the shovel blade, I rammed it down with both hands, again and again, as you would a posthole digger. My hole now had its shape and depth—round, narrower at the top than at the bottom, where, as best I could, I hollowed out a chamber. Jacob would lie in a cavity the shape of an urn or uterus.

None of this was necessary. I might have taken him to the vet's, scratched him behind the ears, and left him there. He had been left there often enough not to be alarmed by it. Harry would do the rest, and dispose of him afterwards. If we wished, he could even arrange for the dog to be cremated. He had given me a booklet explaining such things, called *Parting with Your Pet*. That would be the painless and convenient way to do it, and it was not clear to me why I felt it could not be done that way, since he was dying precisely for the sake of painlessness and convenience. But for the moment the satisfaction of digging the grave seemed solid enough. Deerflies troubled me some; cicadas buzzed, and my eyes blurred with sweat. A killdeer called out from the deep abyss of the August sky. It was hard to think beyond the job at hand, which I now finished. I stood to admire it for a moment, and then walked back up to the house.

There was time for a swim in the river, at the town landing. I went there, dived in, and swam up against the tide a long way, well on toward exhaustion, and drifted lazily back down. That just left time enough to change clothes, pick up the dog, put him into the truck, and drive briskly into town. Harry wanted to do it last thing before he closed for the afternoon. Perhaps this was for the sake of his customers. Even if it is only your canine or feline proxy, and not yourself, you do not like to be reminded that some patients enter hospitals for the purpose of dying.

I left him in the back of the truck. Harry's office is a remodeled house at the edge of town, and he keeps the grounds neatly groomed—petunias line the gravel walkway; cosmos and daisies bloom in the mulched beds that flank the front door. Inside, everything is linoleum and vinyl, but the sense of homeyness is preserved by the two or three friendly assistants who work with Harry each summer. Some are already through veterinary school and are serving a kind of internship; others are just beginning and are gaining early experience in what they plan to be their life's work. Mostly, they are young women, both dedicated and cheerful, good at putting animals and their owners at ease. Harry himself is that way—relaxed, sympathetic, with an air of professional discretion. He has grown himself a fine, full beard, which he keeps carefully trimmed, to emphasize a certain scholarly quality in him. Vets are no longer horse doctors, obstetricians to cows and ewes, gelders of boars and bulls. Their clients are mostly suburban; they are pet doctors, with a professional personality like that of a good pediatrician.

A Pastoral Occasion

🌫

I watched with some amusement as Harry finished with his next-to-last customer of the day, a lady in sandals and sunglasses, who held a groggy, post-operative tomcat in her arms. Post-operative and post-tom too, I gathered. He was assuring her that the cat would hold nothing against her. She plainly doubted him: "Won't he always feel I've deprived him of something?" Harry said no, not at all. The cat would only suffer from a little local discomfort for a couple of days. After that, he'd be as happy as a clam at high tide. She left, holding the cat close to her face, nuzzling it. Harry had once studied to be a priest, and I considered a bad joke, a way to lighten the moment—"So now he's the involuntary Origen of his species." But Harry was busy, his back to me, as he placed a few things quickly, almost furtively, into a narrow black case. He said something to the receptionist about tomorrow's appointments and turned abruptly, with a kind of brusqueness, to me. "Let's go," he said.

It all went quickly now. I lowered the tailgate and crawled up inside the truck. Jacob was trying to rise. I helped him up, and he walked to the edge of the tailgate, his spine humped, his tail wagging the equivalent of the uncertain smile with which you approach a person who may choose not to recognize you. Harry was looking at him, then looked at me. "It's time to do it all right," he said, allowing no second thoughts. It was easy to get the dog to lie down on the tailgate and keep still. I squatted beside him, and rubbed his ears and nape. Harry opened his case, took out a rubber tube, wrapped it around the foreleg, tightened and knotted it. He drew a clear liquid into the syringe, found the vein with his forefinger, and slipped the needle in. An inky spurt of blood, curling and roiled like smoke, appeared in the syringe. Then the slow pressure of the thumb on the plunger, forcing first the blood back into the vein, then the anesthetic. Thirteen years of life figured in that small action—the jet of living blood into the clear fluid, the squeezing of blood and fluid back into the dog.

There was no convulsion or shudder. Almost as soon as the

plunger started forward, the dog's breathing grew easy and unla-
bored. His eyes closed, and the breathing became steadily deeper
and more deliberate. When the plunger was something more than
half advanced, he sighed profoundly, as though after a very good
meal, and stopped breathing. Harry completed the injection,
withdrew the needle, and leaned forward to lift the dog's eyelid
with his thumb—a deft, sacerdotal motion. He seemed satisfied
with what the eye contained, but drew some more fluid into the
syringe. "He's a big fellow," he said. "We'd better play it safe. A
bouncy truck ride can act as artificial respiration." I nodded because
I could not trust my throat to speak. He picked up the limp foreleg, offhandedly this time, jabbed the needle in, and emptied it
quickly.

When I got down from the tailgate and looked up, the day
seemed very bright, as though I had emerged from a cinema in
midafternoon. I started to walk back toward the office with Harry,
to pay the bill, but he touched my shoulder. "Don't bother. We'll
mail it in the morning." I nodded again, and for some reason shook
his hand, and returned to the truck.

As I drove home, I found it possible to remember beyond Jacob's
decrepitude, back to when he had been a valued dog. It was not
like the breaking of a dam—there was no sudden flood of recol-
lections and images. It was rather as though a blocked passage or
interrupted circuit had been cleared, restoring normal commu-
nication. Memory follows certain forms and conventions—the
obvious one of chronology, the less obvious ones that edit your
remembering and fit it to a theme. A dog is not complex—dogs
are what they are from a very early date. They do not change,
and if they surprise you, it is probably because you have been
inattentive. But our gift for complicating our relation to the simplest things is endless, even when we have selected those things
in the hope that they might simplify our selves. The dog was part
of the life I had chosen, with the faith that it might somehow

educate me, lead me out of myself toward a solid world, where things existed, and might be experienced without reflection.

Hunting is an ancient metaphor for this active, unreflective life, for desire in the unheeding pursuit of its object. That is, it is a metaphor for a life in which nothing is metaphoric, and which need not imagine itself in any other 'erms. But I had always owned hunting dogs—pointers, like Jacob, or brittanies or setters—and at some point I noticed that all of them were neurotic, and that this was because of what was expected of them. Their instinct to hunt, to track, stalk, seize, and kill, was simultaneously fostered and frustrated. The dog was always denied the last gratification: it was to point, but not to pounce; to seize the downed bird, but not to devour it. Before Jacob, every hunting dog I owned, good or bad, had had a certain air of hysteria, of pent-up energy that would periodically explode, and render it unmanageable for an hour, or even an entire afternoon of swearing and storming and cajoling. Hunter and dog on such occasions become trite illustrations of superego and id, repressive dictatorship and anarchic mob, each the agent of the other's frenzy. So not even hunting dogs, much less their owners, abandoned themselves to headlong pursuit of the object. When they did, it was something like insanity.

Jacob had none of this. I had picked him from a squirming litter and brought him home. We named him Jacob because his coat— dingy white heavily spotted and ticked with brown—resembled the variety of bean called Jacob's cattle. There had been a jar of them on the kitchen counter when I brought him into the house, and we had looked at the dog, then at the jar, and it had seemed, in a minor way, a sign—here was the obvious name for a puppy who needed one, and who still had the plump shapelessness of a beanbag. Driving home now, I found that time present and available to me as it had not been even an hour before. Elizabeth, not yet two weeks old, lay upstairs in her hamper. Susan's sewing basket was on the kitchen table, filled with scraps of colorful material intended for an infant's quilt. She had hoped to finish it before the baby was born, and felt determined to finish it now, so that Elizabeth might have what you would like each child to have— some labor of love to lie in, something bright and soft to greet its awakening to the world. The puppy whimpered some that first night, and we could hear a certain amount of bumping and scraping from the kitchen, where we had left him in a large box. Next morning we found him out of the box, beside the overturned sewing basket, bedded down in the quilt scraps. He looked at us, his brow furrowed with uncertainty, as though he expected a scolding. Susan laughed—"Maybe we should name you Joseph, with your coat of many colors, and pack you off to Egypt—maybe that's what we'd better do. Is that what you'd like?"

But he remained Jacob, after the clever and conniving supplanter whom he did not particularly resemble. Before he was three months old, it was apparent that his hips were bad, and we had to decide whether or not to keep him. He was brighteyed and endearing, already housebroken, and so we kept him. I felt a misgiving about this, the way you do when you yield to your own tenderheartedness. The hunters I had known in my boyhood doted on their dogs and treated them well, but they would have put down a genetically imperfect one as unhesitatingly as they would have returned a piece of defective merchandise, and with the same sense that their doing so was *pro bono publico* and not merely for themselves. I went ahead and trained him, and we hunted for all but his last two years, despite his progressive infirmity. He was, from the beginning, a melancholy, conscience-stricken dog, with no instinct for play or mischief. It goes without saying that, even in his old age, the sight of the gun and hunting coat excited him, and set him into a geriatric capering around the truck, waiting to be lifted in. But once afield, he was always careful, worried and tentative, as though he suspected a booby trap at every turn. My least show of exasperation demoralized him, and he would simply sit, as though commanded to do so, and refuse to hunt. So I learned to say nothing at all that might inhibit him, and he would move ahead of me with great diffidence, looking back inquiringly every few yards, like a batter checking with the third base coach after each pitch. He had no style at all; he looked like something you might see slinking among overturned garbage cans in an alleyway.

At home, even as a young dog, he was inclined to lie low, and he confined himself to an imaginary kennel that he created in the corner of the kitchen between the stove and the pantry. He seldom left it voluntarily, clinging to it as stubbornly as some of us cling to our self-imposed limitations. The children accepted him as children accept the given circumstances of their lives, and he tolerated them in the same way. But unfamiliar children filled him with consternation, and he would retreat from their overtures into the darkest corner of the kitchen and cower there, growling, his eyes baleful, his tail clapped between his legs. Our friends regarded him as the expression of a self-consciously quirky taste, like a stuffed moose head over the mantel or a pair of plaster flamingos on the lawn, and as an invitation to wit. It became a joke to name him; he was Lazarus, Tithonus, Aeolus of the ill wind, the grim sleeper, Uriah Heep; Cotton Mather and a giraffe were implicated in his ancestry. When company came for supper, he would bark at each new arrival with the implacability of an unattended moralist, and eventually edge up to each person in turn, and sniff suspiciously, and then, his worst expectations confirmed, he would retreat to his corner. There he would sleep loudly, his snoring filling the intervals of conversation. Occasionally I would look over and see him, still tightly curled in his corner, his back to the room, but awake now, his head lifted just enough to glare at me with one reproachful eye. Then he would sigh, shift a little, and resume his sleep. He was like an old family retainer or a poor relation, some vestige of your earlier circumstances, never allowing you to forget that he knew *his* place, and asserting his rights by denying that he had any. But he was quiet and reclusive, seldom much of a nuisance.

Billy Watson's Croker Sack

Hunting was in October, for grouse. They seemed so deeply indigenous to this part of New England that, in hunting them, I felt myself at times infringing on a privilege properly belonging only to natives. Their fondness for apples explains why they haunt old house sites, farms sunk back into forest, and the stone fences that once marked the borders of fields. Further north, they are a true forest bird, but here they have become a bird of abandoned history, as though they had once been domestic fowl, left to fend for themselves when the families moved on to richer lands along the primeval Ohio, or when the young men did not return from Chancellorsville or the Seven Days, Little Round Top or the Bloody Salient. You imagine the birds clinging hard to the deserted farmstead for as long as anything was there—pecking in the earth where the garden was, scratching beneath the rotting sills of the barn for whatever grain had sifted through, filling their gizzards with grit from the road while the road lasted, until slowly the sumacs edged into it, and the alders, and it ceased to be a road. But—sometimes in regular orchards, but much more commonly planted thriftily, along stone fences or at the edge of fields, or on the banks of gullies too steep to mow—the apple trees persisted, renewed themselves, and kept bearing, and the grouse haunted them, elusive and shadowy as fugitives.

A more energetic and exuberant dog would have been an intruder in these places. Jacob was as discreet and somber as an undertaker. Grouse are unalterably wild, and will not hold for a dog as quail or woodcock do. In the thick, overgrown country, you seldom had more than a fleeting glimpse of one, a blurred impression of wings. No matter how diligent the dog, most of our hunts ended without a shot being fired. This did not bother me. I liked the places the birds took us. Looking into an old cellar hole, where a sturdy ash had thrust its way up through the chimney arch, or peering down into the cool, reverberant depths of a well, I had the sense of a history much older than was in fact the case, as though I had been a citizen of the later empire, who had come upon some solid, incontrovertible vestige of the early republic, of a past long since digested into nostalgia and literature. The morose, painstaking dog faded into this scene as a fish dissolves from your sight back down into deep water, and I followed the thin clinking of his collar tags as best as I could.

As he got older and slower, he became more and more effective. Certain trees had a special attraction to grouse, even in years when they were not bearing well, and each of these was a problem to be solved, an approach to be worked out, the dog coming in from one side, perhaps, and the hunter standing off in a small clearing to the other side, in hopes that the bird would flush that way, and afford a shot. The odds still favored the bird, but not so extravagantly as they had done. The dog was methodical, and he knew each place as well as he knew the kitchen, the barn, the yard, and absolutely nothing else. I seldom spoke to him, or whistled him in, or told him his business. He never overran a bird, or failed to find a dead one. Slowly, October after October, I came to feel almost naturalized, if not to the region and the town, then at least to these few bypassed, unvisited spots, where particular apple trees stood and created small clearings in the forest. I could distract insomnia by visualizing each of the four or five farms we hunted regularly, and recalling, individually, each of the birds we had taken there. At some point I realized that he was easily the best hunting dog I had ever owned, but I could hardly boast about him, as he lay curled in his usual corner of the kitchen, as indifferent to our comings and goings as a mule would have been.

By his tenth year, he could not walk a mile without resting, and so we began to hunt by driving as close as possible to the most reliable trees, checking them quickly, and driving on to the next farm and the next tree. This altered our hunting, by depriving the places of their context. It was not exactly like reading an abridged version of a book, or seeing only the most eventful innings of a game; it was more like what happens when you stop trying to remember people or events in their fullness, and content yourself with recalling them as they appear in snapshots, or as they are preserved in some oft-repeated anecdote. But we killed grouse at an unprecedented rate that October. It was Nimrod's daydream—the dog flawless, the bird always at the expected place, the gun unable to miss. Again and again there would be the abrupt explosion of the flush, the shadowy instant when the gun finds the bird even before the mind has registered its image, and then, with no consciousness of having released the safety or pulled the trigger, the bird falling, the solid thump against the ground that makes it real. Jacob would fetch it as he always did, not mangling it or even disturbing its feathers, but powerfully reluctant to let go until I gave his ear a tug, which caused him to drop it abruptly, as though it were hot. The limp weight and dry, dusty smell of the bird were magically accomplished facts, and there would, by a different kind of magic, be a bird in the same place when we returned to it the following week. At the end of the season, I drew a rough map of each of our regular territories, and marked on each map the places where we had gotten grouse, and the date. They had become too many for me to rehearse to myself at night, trying to put myself to sleep. His life's work came to forty-six grouse. There were a good many more woodcock—too many to bother with—but they were only incidental.

By the next October he could scarcely go a hundred yards before his legs gave out. I took him out once, to a woodcock cover close beside the road, but he could not manage even that, so I returned him to the truck and started home. On the way, or not much out of the way, there was a favored apple tree, one of our regular spots. I left him whimpering and barking in the truck. A grouse was there, but it flushed out of range. Walking back to the truck through a cutover area, I flushed and killed a woodcock. It fell into a pile of slash, and search as I might I could not find it. It ended with my going back to the truck, picking up the dog, and lugging him across the logging debris to where the bird had fallen. He smelled it even before I put him down on the slash pile, and, after a moment of noisy rooting and snuffing, he extricated the bird. I put it in my coat, lugged him back to the truck, then returned and got the gun, and that was our last hunt.

From then on he lay, twelve months a year instead of eleven, in the kitchen, beside the stove in summer, under it in winter, struggling up only to eat and to go outside off and on during the day, in his fitful, distracted way, as though looking for something missing. We got Bonnie, an affable young retriever. In the coldest weather the two of them curled into a single lump of dog. He exhibited no jealousy. His eyes faded, although he knew so well, by smell and habit, the kitchen, the barn, and the dooryard, that this seldom inconvenienced him. I only realized how blind he had become one day when he walked squarely into a little wagon that Hannah had left on the back step. It alarmed him, and he sat down and barked at the thing, dogmatic, querulous, not to be placated—a Job whose patience this last small indignity, added to his life's list of afflictions, had broken.

I drove the truck past the house, across the pasture, and to the edge of the slope. The last strong afternoon light fell nearly horizontal across the stubble; the shadow of the house stretched far into the field. The slope itself lay in deep shadow now. Grief, the swelling of the throat and blurring of the eyes, is involuntary, and it is pointless to try to decide when circumstances do or do not justify it. But it surprised me all the same. I opened the tailgate. He lay in a posture resembling sleep, but with the limbs and angle of the head wrong, somehow too slack and lax. It looked like a competent amateur's rendering of a dog—the proportions right, the legs and ears and muzzle all accurately done, and yet no sense of the whole thing as one creature. It was awkward lifting him. His dead weight shifted like sand in a sack, and he was a heavy animal. I had to put him down on his back and drag him by the forelegs the last few yards.

I tried to lower him gently, but he slipped free and flopped down into the grave with a sodden thud. And with that he sighed and grunted softly. It was unmistakable. I felt a kind of horror. Had the truck ride, and this final bump, revived him? It took a certain clench-jawed deliberation not to shovel the dirt down on him immediately, or simply turn and walk away. I made myself watch him closely for what I did not want to see—some fluttering of the eyelid or flexing of the nostril. Nothing seemed to move, but it was dark in the hole, and the signs of life would be very dim. I knelt to peer in more closely, and finally reached my hand down to touch him, as gingerly as you might touch an iron to see if it were hot. The air was dank and chill beneath the earth, but his flank still felt warm. There was no respiration. I pressed the heel of my hand hard against his rib cage. He sighed. So that was all—the fall had forced air from his lungs, as from a bellows. I withdrew my arm and looked at him again. He lay awkwardly, his limbs sprawled, like a dead dog beside the road. I reached back down, turned him on his side, and drew the legs into the curled position natural to any animal at rest. He looked comfortable now, an accurate representation of a sleeping dog.

Impossible not to think of him as he had lain for so many years in his corner, while doors opened and shut, friends entered and left, and the children, growing up, began to come and go. I slowly began shoveling the dry, rubbly clay back into the hole, covering him gradually, moving forward from the hindquarters. When he lay under a blanket of dirt, with only his head and shoulders visible, I looked at him a last time, then looked no more, and shoveled methodically until the grave was filled and mounded. When I stopped, it was suddenly cool in the shadows, and you could feel how the year was turning away toward autumn; but high overhead a few bland clouds still drifted in a placid summer sky. We might set up a stone later, but this would do for now.

5 ✦ Dawn's Early Light

Peter Footer tells me that he and his buddy Jerry went out at high tide the night before, got the gunning float exactly where they wanted it to be, anchored, and spent the night there, sleeping, or at least trying to, in the bottom of the float. By 4 A.M. they were stranded on the mud; then the tide started creeping back. When daylight came, they were all set, and had that corner of the marsh to themselves. "So how'd you do?" I ask Peter. "Nothing special," says Peter. "A black came in early, and Jerry got him. Then it was just teal. We let 'em set in the decoys, hopin' for another black or a mallard. 'Bout 8:30 or 9:00 I says to him, 'Looks like it's teal or nothing,' so he shot two teal and I got my three and that was it. All greenwings."

I got my limit of teal on opening day, too, and with less effort. I got up shortly after three, cooked breakfast, ate, and went out with the dog into the dark. The canoe was on the truck; the gun, shells, and half a dozen rough decoys were already inside it. Twenty minutes of driving; another twenty of paddling. I'd scouted the afternoon before, had seen where I wanted to be, and had memorized the silhouette of the tree line behind the marsh. That was what I used to navigate by now. I paddled in toward the trees until I ran out of water, placed the decoys in a small channel, and slid the empty canoe on into shore. We were still early, so Bonnie and I sat there and waited. We could hear boats motoring up or down the Bay, and see, here and there in the darkness, the brief winking of flashlights. Once or twice I clicked on my own light, to let late-comers know that this territory was taken. When the stars began to fade, we waded out and took our stand. The water was ankle deep now, infiltrating the grass as surreptitiously as the light seeping into the sky. An owl floated over, headed for the woods—night's watchman calling it a day. Then the first ducks, momentarily visible as a blacker blackness on whistling wings.

Further out, I heard blacks or mallards chuckling and guffawing, affable and commonplace as any barnyard ducks. But where I was, as I had expected, there were only teal—an occasional guttural and muted monosyllabic grunt, an equally diffident piping whistle. As the darkness grew opaque, six came out of it, deft, twisting, and sudden as a covey of shooting stars. They splashed down into the decoys; Bonnie whimpered and shivered, and they whirred up from the water, invisible until they cleared the tree line. Off to my right, somebody shot, still ten minutes before the legal opening. Five minutes later, the shooting became general— a steady *whump, whump, whump* from downstream, where the river marshes broadened out into the Bay; the sudden clap of sound from a gunner closer at hand. For the first half hour, things were slow where I was, but I told myself that I had expected that too— the ducks would come here, into this quiet pocket of marsh, as the tide slid up. The dog was worried, eager, anxious, afraid that life was passing her by.

But it did not. I had my limit of three teal by eight o'clock; by nine, I was standing in front of undergraduates, who still wore the frowzy, vulnerable look of sleep, and blathering earnestly about variation and parataxis in the Old English lyric. The day faded on into ordinariness; it would regain a little of its special quality only after supper, when I would go out into the barn, pluck the teal and dress them, watched with furtive and glowering importunity by Mink and Mrs. Pino, our two semi-domestic cats. Then would clean the gun, swabbing out the barrels until they shone like mirrors when I held them to the light and looked through them. Would carefully save a few of the flank feathers and a wing for trout flies; would reward the cats with a visceral morsel; would wrap and label the ducks and put them in the freezer. That would be it, an annual observance completed.

Nobody can make a more compelling case against this kind of thing than the one I regularly make against myself. Leaving aside the generic arguments against hunting, there are specific arguments against duck-hunting. I know how other creatures—deer and grouse, quail and rabbits—endure only one hunting season per annum, and it generally lasts no more than a month or six weeks. For the whole of that season, these animals have the home-field advantage. They know where the food is, where the shelter is; they are street-wise and flexible, and can melt into their land-scapes like ghosts or guerrillas. But ducks arrive like refugees, driven by weather, caught by sudden freeze-ups, pursued by the annual calamity of winter—many would die if there were no hunters at all. And they must run a gauntlet of overlapping seasons, one that begins in September in Canada and extends to Florida and January. Beyond those killed or crippled by hunters there are the ones that die from hunger and fatigue, because the shooting has driven them from their resting and feeding places, and they have no reserves of energy or fat. Every duck-hunter has known days, usually late in the season after the weather has turned bitter, when ducks will come in to decoys like moths to a flame. You tend to regard these days as restitution for all the times when you had hunkered in the blind and the birds, maddeningly circumspect, stayed beyond range. But those are also the days when you are glad that the law sets a limit on how many you can kill. If it did not, you would have to resist on your own the temptation we can hardly bear to acknowledge—the one posed by another creature's complete vulnerability.

One year I tried a compromise. Summer ended; Bonnie pranced with the flirtatious expectancy that seems to seize so many animals when the first frosts come; and the ducks began arriving on the Bay. But I slept late on opening day, went to work, and postponed delinquency until mid-afternoon. It was low tide then, and I took the dog and we walked over the mudflats. I had the gun, but did not need it. In less than an hour, she rooted out three ducks that had been crippled in the morning barrage, and I returned home before dark with my limit, a clear conscience, and a strong sense of polluted ritual. Next year, and all the years after that— at least all of them so far—I kept the custom in my regular way. If I had a yaller dog, and he was as noisy and useless as my conscience has proven itself to be on this subject, I would, as Huck Finn says, "pison him." But I have a black dog, and every October her eyes brighten with a vivid, unquenchable, and communicable enthusiasm for the unconscionable.

I admire the inefficiency of the way Peter Footer got his limit. He and I are the same age, and it is an age at which lying in a sleeping bag on the floor of an open boat, feeling your joints congeal and your bones ache in the dankness, does not recommend itself. I suppose he started duck-hunting about the same time I did, when he was nine or ten years old. He still lives on a remnant of the farm where he grew up, and where his father grew up, down along the big marshes at the Androscoggin mouth. And that was how they did it, every year—went out to lay claim to their particular patch of marsh on the night before the season opened.

Think about it—about lying out under the starry diagrams, in the middle of a tidal marsh, waiting, drifting asleep, coming back awake. Time and tide are not abstractions; they are over your head and all around you, and you can see, hear, and feel them working through the night. As the water ebbs out of the marsh, the wild rice and bulrushes emerge, but not in the same way that they push up out of the mudflats every spring. First they bend, their heavy heads held by the surface tension of the water. When the tide is half out, most of them are still prostrate, and then the resiliency of the stalks begins to assert itself. The stem breaks free first, and bows itself up into a shallow arch; it appears to be rooted at both ends. The tide drops further, the loft and tension of the arch increase, and finally the tasselled head lifts out of the water. The plant does not straighten up suddenly, like a bent branch springing back into place. The head hangs just above the surface, with droplets falling singly from it, lightening it, allowing it gradually to rise in a slow-motion upward swoon. In the bottom of the boat, you do not hear so much as feel a rustling, whispering hush of stirring reeds all around you, and the small metronymic plinking, drop by drop by drop, of water into water. Early in the night, looking north up the Bay, you see the Dipper in its familiar autumnal alignment, more or less horizontal, its handle pointing west. As the night passes, the handle rotates slowly counterclockwise; if you wake in the small hours to see what time it is and listen for the first ducks, you see the Dipper straight up. The last star in the handle is barely above the tree line, and the whole constellation looms over you, portentous as an illuminated clock face in a darkened room.

You are not to imagine that Peter Footer spoke to me about these things. He after all is a Maine carpenter, one of the kind upon whom other Maine carpenters bestow their ultimate accolade: "That Peet-ha is *some* fussy." He was recommended to us, and we hired him this past summer, to restore our mudroom. Sometimes, watching him working away at rotten sills and collapsed foundations, I felt like we'd hired a diamond cutter to mine coal. But thrift is part of the moral aesthetic of a craftsman; the work was done within budget and it was done on time, which is to say that it was completed well before Opening Day. Susan and I were more than satisfied by what he had done, and our satisfaction with the work is enhanced by our memory of the workman. Once during the summer I went to a local lumberyard, to get a few planks for a project of my own, and the manager in the yard said to me: "I believe Peter Footer's putting down a floor for you. He was in here picking out the boards for it last week. Now I don't mind a fellow that's choosy going through a pile of lumber. But Peter is something else. Swear to God, when he goes through a pile, he don't *select* the boards; he *interviews* 'em. Individually and at length. I could get married and buy a house, get divorced and sell it, and not worry about it as much as he does buying three hundred foot of number two pine, and you can tell him I said that. He'll consider it a compliment."

So Peter Footer isn't a man who spent the night out on the Bay because he has the sort of casual and laid-back temperament that doesn't calculate the ratio of effort to result. He does things once, and does them neatly, and does them right. Late this fall, I was back out at the lumberyard, this time to replace a ladder, and there he was, forking through a stack of lumber, testy and skeptical as my mother rifling through a pile of fabrics in a dry goods store. "You'll have to do, I guess," he'd say to one plank; "Not you; not you; not you," to the next three. I laughed and said he looked like St. Peter himself, deciding who got admitted and who didn't. "At least what St. Peter turns away'll burn," he said. "I'm not so sure I'd want to say that much for some of this stuff." We fell to talking, and that was when he told me about how he got the three teal on Opening Day. He was a little embarrassed about it, and yet he wanted to talk about it too, because it didn't make sense, not according to the standards he used to make sense of the rest of his life. "I know there's better ways to do it," he said. "I guess I'm a glutton for punishment. Every year I tell myself that next year I'll take it easy. And even when I tell myself that, I know that next year me and Jerry or some other fool will be right out there again. So then I tell myself, 'Footer, looks like you're afraid that if you started getting smarter, it might mean you was getting older.' "

My rituals and vigils for Opening Day are less than his, but no less irremediable. Apart from the one year when the dog and I went out and gleaned cripples, there has been a steady tendency for me to leave the house and reach the marsh earlier and earlier. That is how I know about the sighing and dripping of the reeds in the dark, and the way the Big Dipper swings around to stand on its handle above the northern horizon. What is hard to explain, even to myself, is why that wonderful experience of waiting for dawn on Merrymeeting Bay has to be linked to duck-hunting, and particularly to the first day of the season. Of course hunting richly satisfies the craving for suspense and excitement; and I would be lying if I did not also mention the satisfaction of handling again a gun that I have owned for thirty years, and of that sweet, compact motion, which must be made without hesitation or adjustment, that overtakes the duck in flight, pushes the barrels ahead of the bird, and kills it cleanly. But those are not the primary things. The primary things always seem elusive, indistinct, shadowy— more like the arrowy shapes that come whistling out of the dark before shooting time than like the solid, ponderable bird—drake or hen, wood duck, teal, black, or mallard—that you can take from the good dog's mouth, admire for a moment, and put into your coat. I have an idea that many of the things we do may be like that—more important in their incidental details and acciden- tal associations than at the center, and most important at the remotest boundaries, where your conscious, finite purpose draws its nourishment from unrealized or half-realized impulses and memories.

Late in one stubborn, unyielding winter a good many years ago, I undertook to make some decoys for myself, using spruce two-by-eights that were lying around in the barn, and working with a hatchet, pocket-knife, and rasp. They came out looking crude and blocky—a friend picked one up, scrutinized it from several angles, and said it betrayed an imperfectly assimilated Cubist influence—yet they have always done the job. Ducks don't seem to have much of an eye for detail. But I don't take any satisfaction in these merely workmanlike effigies. In the fashioning of them, I had begun to realize that my motives were not practical. Cheap and perfectly serviceable plastic ones were available. The motive was more Pygmalion like—to give shape to a longing.

When you try to make almost anything, you are probably working in a tradition, whether you know it or not. It is almost more interesting not to know it, and only belatedly come to see that the tradition was working in you before you were conscious of yourself working in it. A considerable time after I had completed my clunky specimens, I began looking a little bit into decoy-making, and found that its Golden Age had been from about 1880 to 1920. In the past quarter-century or so, the classifying, authenticating, and collecting of decoys of this vintage has become a big business, very far removed from the salt marshes and tide flats. Recently, the market seems to have declined slightly, but a local dealer tells me that plenty of wooden ducks out there are still bringing what he called "serious money"—$10,000 and upward. And he told me that in 1986, at an auction in Kennebunk, Maine, a pintail made of white pine sold for $319,000, which is the highest price ever paid for a piece of American folk art.

The prices are incidental, and even accidental. The decoys were made to fool ducks, and to cost two or three dollars apiece. You need to look at them that way, as things of use, almost always made by men who gave them that use, and plenty of it. These old decoys vary in style, but they all have in common a precision that is far in excess of a duck's apparent powers of discrimination. Even with all the paint worn off, a redhead decoy is recognizable by its high forehead, a widgeon by its slightly undersized bill. Regardless of species, and somewhat at odds with strict verisimilitude, there is an exaggerated shapeliness usually evident in the curve of the neck and the arch of the back. A good decoy has fine lines in the same way that a good boat does. It looks as though it had been smoothed and molded into existence by a potter, and invites handling.

The $319,000 pintail was made by Elmer Crowell, of East Harwich, Massachusetts. I am not myself convinced that it represents the finest of his work. Although I have only seen his decoys in photographs, the most remarkable to me is of a black duck. It is reaching its head back to preen itself. One wing-tip is slightly elevated, and it gives the bird the asymmetrical tension and poised imbalance of a cantilevered building. You would not think of it as folk art; you would think of it as something that was made to be exhibited on its own small pedestal, in the shadowless light of a bare, silent room. But Crowell was a guide; decoys were his sideline. And even the guiding was a secondary and subsidiary activity—he had become a pusher purely in order to support his habit, which was duck-hunting. He shot ducks commercially until Federal regulation put him out of business, and hunted for sport thereafter, although he preferred the old days of unrestricted slaughter—the sink-box, the swivel gun, the night hunting. You would expect his decoys to be simple, sturdy, and inexpensive, given his businesslike approach to waterfowling. They never were, and in fact had a poor reputation among hunters. He seems often to have used imperfectly cured pine—Peter Footer would have been scandalized—and many of his birds split or checked when subjected to the constant wetting and drying, freezing and thawing of field conditions. The fineness of carving that characterized even his earliest birds meant that the heads, necks, and bills broke too easily, given the rough, offhand treatment that decoys inevitably get.

Crowell looks to me like an extreme case, but not an atypical one. The art of the decoy began to flourish during the final decades of a massacre of migratory birds that was without precedent, and that can never be repeated. The flocks that flowed north and south, spring and fall, will not be seen on this planet again. What you see instead is a dusty, eyeless scaup or scoter sitting in a dealer's showroom, wearing a price that makes you flinch. It was made by and for the men who participated enthusiastically, and often professionally, in the massacre. The astonishing thing is that the men had such an accurate appreciation for the individual grace, beauty, and proportion of the birds they slaughtered so wantonly. They became artists without intending to. The ducks, on their way out, decoyed the hunters.

Duck art and duck kitsch—mallard-headed door knockers, coat hangers, umbrella handles, faucets; canvasback-embossed door mats, bath mats, hearth rugs, lampshades, platters, saucers, ice buckets—are everywhere. No other animal has such a broad-based totemic potency. Eighty or a hundred years ago, all up and down the Atlantic coast, you would have found men who were, socio-economically if not artistically, the equivalents of Elmer Crowell. They no doubt did all kinds of seasonal work—crabbed, clammed, lobstered, oystered, seined, fished—but what they lived for, whether as market hunters or as guides, was the arrival of cold weather and the first waves of ducks. They were not men of property. Their tradition of hunting, to the extent that it owed anything to England, derived from the unlanded underclass of rural society—men who were poachers, practical and sly, handy with boats, nets, guns, dogs, traps, and snares. They were excluded from the English tradition of hunting, which was restricted by law to men of substantial property. In the unbounded space of the New World, they founded the American tradition. Their own range was gradually squeezed and shrunken; one of their last habitats was one of the stubbornest frontiers of all—the intertidal zone of marshes, mudflats, and swamps that were legally and literally no man's land.

When I sit in a den that is all gussied up in the rustic-elegiac,

pseudo-outdoorsy Ralph Lauren manner, and see over the mantel-
piece a limited edition print, signed by the artist, of black ducks
dropping into a tawny salt marsh ("Winter Wings"), I feel something complicated. Duck-hunting has become a rich man's sport,
and the print probably hangs there chiefly as an assertion of status. In that respect, it means about what a fox-hunting print would
mean in an equivalent English household. But there is a differ-
ence. In the fox-hunting print, we see, in the foreground, the
human pageant and drama: crop-tailed horses and red-coated rid-
ers clearing a hedge or sunken lane in impeccable style. We con-
template their skill, their equipage, and especially the majestic,
wooden-faced, definitively British imperturbability with which the
hunters pursue their quarry, as though they did not so much intend
to kill the fox as to *cut him dead*. Off in the middle distance, we see
what they are riding toward—a horse standing quietly, a circle of
hounds, a man in the center of it, holding up something scruffy.
It could as well be a squirrel or cat. The duck painting, by contrast, focuses on the birds themselves. The perspective is like that
of a formal portrait: the ducks, filling the foreground, exceed the
dimension of biology. The landscape behind them—the marshes,
water, and sky—implies and subserves their power. While the
painting may be no more than a status object, it nevertheless
removes you completely from your human context. The image
celebrates space, freedom, and wildness—the heritage of the
unclaimed continent. Pretension is a kind of hypocrisy and
hypocrisy is a kind of homage. If you even want to pose as a duck
hunter, you must at least pretend to still see the beauty and potency
of the birds. And, whether you know it or not, that is a way of
claiming kinship with the old guides and decoy-makers, who chose
to live marginally—at the margins of society and in the margin of
unpossessed earth that still existed between the tides.

When I was all of fourteen, I stood beside an old man, whom I
knew only as Robert, on a dike separating marshes that had once

been ricefields. I now have some perfectly conventional and ordinary understanding of that scene. I was a white boy; he was a black man, old enough to be at least my grandfather. His own grandfather undoubtedly spent his life digging and maintaining the ditches that were still visible in the marsh. He called my father, who was half his age, *captain*, pronouncing it very short: *cap'm*. He avoided calling me anything. I called him Robert, but also *sir*. I did not know if that was right or not, and he gave me no clue. In general, you were to *sir* and *ma'am* all adults, but the rules weren't clear as they pertained to black adults. That perplexed me—I liked the uniform anonymity of manners; you could hide behind them. In Robert's case, I thought *sir* the proper thing. Coming down in the car, I had heard Daddy and the others talking about him, and had heard a sort of careful respect in their voices. He had met us at the landing, thin, stooped, and taciturn. He wore hip boots shucked over at the knee. Most men clump around awkwardly in hip boots, but he moved as comfortably in them as in a pair of old slippers.

It was a great treat and a privilege to hunt the place we were hunting. It belonged to a man who was rich enough to own it and generous enough to ask Daddy down, and to tell him to bring me along. But I did not think about that. I certainly did not think about the history and the historical attitudes that were implicit in these diked and ditched marshes, and in the quandries of etiquette that arose when I spoke to Robert. The abandoned ricefields we looked over, the distant line of swamp trees or pines on the highland, existed in my consciousness in exactly the same way that the marshes, sky, and water exist in "Winter Wings." They were accessories to ducks, the medium in which duck-hunting took place.

Robert paddled two men out into the marsh, placed them in a blind, came back, got me and Daddy, and took us to another blind. There had been a lot of talk at the landing about somebody who wasn't there yet. I hadn't paid any attention, but now it turned out that when this man arrived, Robert would bring him out to join us in the blind. Three in a blind is too many. So, when the man arrived, Daddy and I had already talked it over, and it was clear that I, being the youngest and a poor shot to boot, should go back to the bank. I could squirrel-hunt, and, along the edges of the marsh, there would at least be the theoretical chance of a duck. The man, whose name meant nothing to me, got into the blind, and I got into the boat with Robert. Daddy explained what we were doing to Robert, who simply nodded. As we started out, I picked up a paddle to help him, but he said to put it down; we'd do a little jump shooting before we went in.

I was nervous about that. I had done very little jump shooting, and, given a choice, would rather have paddled than shot. I thought of myself as a pretty good paddler, and knew what kind of a shot I was, especially if there were spectators present. But I couldn't very well trade places with Robert, although it might have been the logical thing to do. As he paddled, I could see at least some of the reason why he was spoken of so respectfully. The boat moved along smoothly; the blade of the paddle never left the water; there was not even the faintest splashing or thumping. At times he would slow down almost to a stop, then thrust the boat ahead, with the bow perhaps angling slightly to the right, and there to the left the ditch would open out into a small pocket or drain, the kind of place where ducks might be lying up. He never said anything, but I could always tell when we were approaching what he thought of as a likely spot, and I would tighten up, more in fear than hope, and feel a shameful relief when nothing was there. Once ripples spread out on the water ahead of us, at a bend in the ditch, and I got myself ready, but when we reached the corner, there was a flurry in the marsh beside the ditch, and a squawk: coot. He flapped and scampered down the ditch, making a scandalous commotion after all our tense silence. Robert chuck-led to himself; "Bluepete," he said.

The afternoon wore on. He could at any point have taken me to shore, left me to hunt squirrels, and relaxed until it was time to go out and pick up the hunters. But he kept on paddling through the broken grid of ditches, and in almost every ditch we seemed to be checking out one or two specific locations that he had some reason to believe were promising. We never jumped anything except the coot, but he didn't get sloppy or casual. Meanwhile, in the next field, we were beginning to hear a good deal of shooting, but none from the blinds behind us, where Daddy and the others were. My own mind began to wander; still on duck-hunting, but now more and more in that territory of daydream that lies just adjacent to the country you actually hunt or fish.

Probably the result would have been the same if I had been more completely where I was. He paused, thrust the boat quickly through a screen of marsh, bow angled slightly to the right, and this time they were there—a pummelling flustration of wings, four big shapes in the air, exactly where they should be, off to my left and close. I was blaming myself for not being ready, for not deserving to hit them, for missing them, even before I shot. And then I had shot twice and was sitting on the front seat of the boat, abject and empty, watching four mallards growing smaller and smaller in the sky.

There was no excuse for it. I didn't know what to say. If I had been alone, at least I could have cursed myself. He had done it all just right. And I knew the next time I shot I would miss again, if there was a next time. My shooting had probably flushed any other ducks that were in this field. I hoped it had. I turned around and apologized. His face showed nothing; he said it was all right. It came out like one word: "Dasserite."

He paddled us briskly on down that ditch to a bigger one—a canal really—that paralleled the dike. We went some distance and then he pulled over, held the boat steady, told me to get out onto the dike, and got out himself. "We gwine cross heah," he said. "Kinder hump down a little." I did what he said, but I didn't like it. The field beyond the dike was almost famous. It belonged to somebody who was always referred to as Vanderbilt—not, as I now realize, because he was a Vanderbilt, but because he was a Yankee of reputedly unlimited wealth and lavish tastes. Also reputed to have bought off the wardens, so that he could bait his field with corn, and ensure that the ducks came to him. And known for a fact to have a caretaker—a man named Bessinger—who was cunning, zealous, and ferocious in dealing with poachers.

Once across, we crouched in a small fringe of marsh between the dike and a ditch that ran along it. Nothing happened; apparently nobody had seen us. "Ain't we trespassing here?" I asked him. He was watching the horizon, and didn't deign to answer right away. Then he turned to me, and spoke with a kind of sternness: "A man is innercent til caught. Dat de law. Yo' daddy a lawyer; you oughter know dat. Now look sha'p." So I looked too, and at first could see only the same empty sky the mallards had left, then, far out across the field, a string of ducks pitching down, and then another. I started to point them out to him, but he said *mack*, which meant nothing to me, and then said it again, very low and urgent, *mack, mack*.

I looked where he was looking, below the tree line and to our right, and there were ducks, ten or twelve of them, not strung out the way ducks usually are, but in a tight clot. They were flying parallel to the dike and headed our way, but they were too far out over the field; they were going to pass by us out of range. But then he did something—he whistled. Three notes, low and distinct: *whew, whew, whew*. The ducks swerved toward us; it was as though Robert had them on a leash. They cupped their wings. "Stan' up," he said. I stood and they flared. I shot vaguely at the lead bird, thinking that when I missed this time I would at least have the law on my side. The bird behind the lead bird crumpled and fell, and the flock banked away from us. As they did, a second duck, as a kind of afterthought, dropped into the water. "Dat fo' de one you miss back yond," Robert said. "Shoot 'em agin; 'e ain' ded yet." So I shot him again, and he was still.

Robert got up then, walked over to the boat, got out a paddle, and came back. He pulled up his hip boots and buckled the straps to his belt, then stepped into the ditch, feeling gingerly with his foot. He started across the ditch, going sideways, and using the paddle as a staff. It was a log, I realized—a log a foot or so beneath the surface, that made a sunken bridge for him to cross on. He got to the marsh on the other side and picked up the ducks. He hooked their heads under his belt, so he could have both hands free, then came back, sidling along the log. He didn't look dottery or unsure, just extra careful.

He laid the birds down on the dike; widgeon, a hen and a drake. We were standing on the crest of the dike, silhouetted against the sky. There was a volley of shots from the Vanderbilt field and some shouting. We looked that way. Far out in the middle of the field a man was standing, so that his head and shoulders were visible above the blind, and yelling at us. You couldn't make out what he was saying, but it wasn't hard to guess. "Look lak it about quittin' time," Robert said, and picked up the ducks. But he didn't go immediately to the boat. He stood in plain sight on the dike, paying no more heed to the man than he would have to a yapping dog. Ducks were beginning to move now, big vees and lines of them up high, far beyond range, headed down to Winyah Bay or wherever it was they went for the night. They did that late every afternoon. Robert studied them as though he expected to recognize some of them individually. He was proving something, standing there like that while the Vanderbilt man yelled at him. 'Gawd mek dem duck for we all, not for he only," he said to me. "Now lessus go."

When I was little, I was irregularly sick. It wasn't anything alarming, just a sort of chronic wheeziness and puniness. Then, in the fifth grade, I got regularly sick, and spent two weeks at a children's hospital outside Wilmington, North Carolina, followed by months at home in bed. At first the shades in my room were down and the curtains were drawn; I was supposed to sleep or lie quietly, and not even get up for meals. After a month of that, I was taken back up to North Carolina for evaluation, and when I returned to Conway, I was allowed to have the shades up and the curtains open, and to sit up in bed and read or draw. That was how the time passed. Every month I would go back to the hospital. The doctor would sit, his head cocked like a robin, taking my pulse, listening to my heart. Blood would be drawn and analyzed, and each time I came back home, it would be with some further restoration of my rights and privileges. By the middle of spring, I was allowed to go outdoors on fine days, and sit on a pallet underneath a big pine in the front yard, where, like Ferdinand the Bull, I could smell flowers and grass again. By midsummer, I had more or less regained the full enfranchisement of my boyhood.

But it was a hard year of waiting. The previous year, I had killed my first duck. The gun I used was a little .410 double barrel, lent to me by my godfather, Mr. C. C. Harper. He had showed up with Daddy one afternoon right before Christmas, and we had driven over to a place that no longer exists, a pond set in scrub oaks and sand dunes, just in off the beach. We put out decoys, and sat and waited. Daddy talked about hunting this same pond when he was about my age or a little older, back when you could use live decoys and the limit was twenty-five. Somewhere in the middle of that talk, there came a sound like the ripping of a bedsheet over our heads and we looked up and here were twenty-five or thirty ringnecks in a tight flock, their wings already set, pitching into the pond. They hit the water with a swoosh, skidded to a stop, composed themselves into a flotilla, and began swimming toward us. They were diving as they came, bobbing back up, uncannily dry, and usually with a bit of pondweed in their bills. Daddy said sit still, and I did. Then, when they were well within the range of even a .410, he whispered to me that I should pick out the closest one and wait for it to dive. When it dived, I was to stand up carefully, and shoot it when it came back up. I did. Then, as the ducks were flushing, Daddy and Mr. Harper each got one. It was unethical for a grown man to shoot a sitting duck. My bird was a drake, chunky and handsome, the first wild duck I had ever seen up close, or held in my hand.

Later in that season, Daddy, Mr. Harper, and a few other men acquired hunting privileges to the ricefields at Chicora plantation. Chicora was owned by Mrs. Wilson, a widow for whom Daddy had done some legal work, pertaining to her husband's estate. She liked and trusted him enough to lease the hunting rights for a price Daddy and the others felt they could afford. Conway was starting to grow a little; the habits created by the Depression and the War were loosening, and a small margin of prosperity, a cautious sense of what you might call disposable income, was beginning to establish itself. Now that I was old enough to hunt, Daddy wanted me to have the experience of going down to the ricefields and touching that figment of an old, ample life. But I got sick instead.

Naturally, Daddy, Mr. Harper, and the others went ahead and hunted Chicora the year I was sick. They went on Opening Day and on as many Saturdays thereafter as they could manage. They would leave in the small hours, and not be back until well after dark. I read a great deal, books I understood and books I didn't: fiction, biographies of famous Americans intended for Youthful Readers, and many stories, invariably sad, about a fox named Vulpes, a mink named Mustela, or an otter named Lutra, as it came blind and squirming into the world, eluded hawks and owls, learned to hunt and hide, felt strange promptings and stirrings in itself on frosty autumnal nights, fought, mated, outsmarted trappers (perhaps losing a toe in the process), and finally, its solitude and wildness uncompromised, succumbed. I read, with a great sense of virtue and 80 percent incomprehension, some volumes of Samuel Eliot Morrison's *History of United States Naval Operations in the Second World War*: the heroic futility of the torpedo bombers at Midway; the Marianas Turkey Shoot; 31 Knot Burke; Ironbottom Sound; the Tokyo Express. But more than anything else, I turned again and again through the pages of Audubon's *Birds of America*. It became one of those superstitious routines of childhood that you do so compulsively that it can almost make you sick. The birds assumed personalities, threatening or beseeching. Even the sequence of the plates seemed to have a significance, although I could not have said what it was.

On days when Daddy and Mr. Harper had gone down to the ricefields, I would pass my time in the usual ways, but also with a kind of Christmas-eve excitement, waiting on them to get back. I knew the schedule of their day—in the blind before dawn, staying there until midmorning, then jump shooting the ditches; finding a good sunny spot for lunch and a bit of a nap, maybe fishing a little with live bait around the ditch-mouths to kill the early afternoon before returning to the blind. By the time I was having my supper and the street lights were coming on, they would be picking up the decoys, calling it quits. They would paddle out of the ditches into the creek, crank up the outboard, and motor down the creek to the Pee Dee, across the Pee Dee to the landing at Chicora. They would load the boat into the truck, take off their hip boots and put on ordinary shoes, so that they could walk up onto the porch of the big house and knock on Mrs. Wilson's door. Her dog would bark until she spoke to it, and they would wait on her to make her way to the door. She would open it, they would step inside just long enough to thank her for the hunt, tell her what they had seen and shot. They would offer her a duck, which she would decline; she would offer them a glass of sherry, which they would decline. Then the long drive back: out to the highway at Plantersville, across the Big Pee Dee bridge and the long, rattling wooden trestle over the swamps at Yauhannah, past Bucksport and Bucksville and Toddville, and on in to Conway. Daddy would generally swing by to drop Mr. Harper off, would be invited in for a drink which would not be sherry and not be declined, and then at last I would hear him turning into the driveway. The truck door would slam shut, and he would come in the kitchen door, speak to Mama, call out to Coles, and come down the hall. He would open my door softly, to see if I was sleeping, find that of course I was not, and ask how I was feeling. "Fine," I'd say. "What did you get?"

When he came into the room, he would still have on his hunting coat. You could smell the cold, outdoor energy of winter in its folds, and also the complex smell—fresh and musty at the same time—of the river marshes. He would spread the coat over the foot of the bed, take the ducks out of the game pouch, and lay them on the coat—four if it had been a good day; on bad days, a measly teal or scaup. Their feathers were ruffled and unkempt; there was a dark gel where the eye had been; a wing or leg might be broken and twisted. I doubt that the elders ever stared at Susannah with any greater rapture and confusion than I stared at those ducks.

It was nothing to do with the triumph of killing them, the hankering for manliness. You could take the tip of a black duck's wing, and open out the wing like a hand of cards. There, just as Audubon had showed it, would be the deep, heartbreaking blue of the speculum against the brown of the wing. The underside of the wing was pure white; the legs a coral red. The breast and belly were the dark umber that gives the bird its name, but the name does not suggest how each dark feather is outlined with a faint marginal trimming of ochre. The whole bird had a lovely, sober look of deliberate understatement, and the traditional name for it in the ricefields was English mallard. That was ornithologically illogical—black ducks are closely related to mallards, but they do not occur in England at all. I can only imagine some homesick colonist looked at one—the prime ricefield bird, big and exceptionally wary, and with such a well-bred, unflashy, unflighty appearance—and thought, by some strange, xenophobic process of poetic associations, of his own, his native land.

The beauty of the ducks that Daddy brought home—widgeon, pintail, teal, mallard, black duck, wood duck—had not been surprising in Audubon's paintings. A painting intends to be beautiful; the only necessities it acknowledges are aesthetic. But it was breathtaking to see, in the actual flesh and feathers, how the slim, tapering sprig of white curved from the drake pintail's breast up the sides of its neck, accentuating the rich brown of the throat, nape, and head, and providing a deft anterior counterpart to the long, slender tail that gives the bird its name and its unmistakable profile in flight. And even a pintail was eclipsed by the drake wood duck, the commonest of all the ricefield ducks. Audubon shows two pairs of them. In the upper half of the painting, just left of center, a drake stands, puffed up and proud, on a sycamore limb; a hen reaches up to him, touching her beak to his. Her wings are aflutter; she is wooing him. In the lower half, just right of center, a hen sits, with only her head and shoulders visible, on her nest in a hollow branch; a drake flies past what is in effect her threshold, crying out. He is now the one who looks eager, joyous, and suppliant. The painting could be called *Courtship and Marriage*, or it could be seen in the light of Audubon's own dandified masculine vanity and his passionate uxoriousness. But he was responding to something that others also saw in the bird. Linnaeus, who probably never set eyes on a live one, was atypically unclinical in giving an official name to this exotic little duck: *aix sponsa*:—bridal duck. I could not believe the first one Daddy brought home—a wild creature, swift and elusive and wonderfully suited to its preferred habitat of swamps and backwaters, with an oriental opulence of plumage. Once in Sunday school we were asked what we would have presented to the infant Jesus in the stable, if we had gone there. The right answer turned out to be a pure heart, or something along those lines, but I knew inside myself that it would be a pair of wood duck, bright and friendly as the ones Audubon had painted.

When I hunt now, it is always just myself and the dog. It had been a more convivial sport when I was growing up. There would only be one other man in the boat or blind, but generally the two of you would be members of a party that would total six or eight in all. A trip to the ricefields was an occasion, an expedition. As a practical matter, you needed enough hunters to cover several hundred acres of marsh. But there was something else, some taste of ritual or re-enactment. Ducks were no longer numerous; you could hunt the ricefields hard all day long and not necessarily get a shot. But all the men of my father's generation had known the wild abundance of that country, when you would go down for two or three days, and might reasonably expect to kill a dozen ducks a day. It hadn't been a time of material amenities or sophisticated recreations, but when the great flocks arrived in November, an older man would round up Daddy and a lot of his friends, and off they would go. They might stay in somebody's cabin or camp out. There would be hearty eating, as much drinking as was commensurate with the serious and strenuous business of hunting, and much telling of stories. You always have that—the telling of stories—in places where there isn't a lot of mobility, but where there is something like hunting: an activity that still has a stylized, carefully preserved flavor of the life of salutary hardship and heroic adventure about it. Paddle a boat through the crinkling skim ice of a ricefield ditch some cold December morning an hour or two before sunrise, and you'll see what I mean. And if in the little pond you are headed toward, there is an eruption of hoarse, raucous mallard-gabble, you will find yourself whispering what was Mr. C. C. Harper's favorite oath: *Great Day. Gah-RATE Day in the MORN-in'.*

By the time I came along, the stories and the hunting had achieved a condition of symbiosis; neither would have survived without the other. Daddy, Mr. Harper, Mr. E. R. McIver (father to my friend Ricky) and Mr. Ned Cox always got into stories after supper, and each man would have his own style of telling them— a way of interrupting himself with his own abrupt laughter, as Mr. McIver did; or of describing the most outrageous absurdities in a mild and plaintive tone, as Mr. Cox did; or Daddy's way of telling a story dialogue-wise, imitating accents and voices. The stories enlarged and enriched the country we hunted, and wouldn't have sounded right anywhere else. It wasn't that they were coarse, and certainly not that they were boastful—boasting had no place in them. But they were free, unconstrained; they made a world where life was comic and unself-conscious, and nobody needed to stand on dignity or hide behind it.

Solidly or precariously, the men who told the stories belonged to the middle class of a small community. There are worse fates. But propriety, conformity, and regularity of behavior were the conditions of that existence. In the ricefields, there were the great open reaches of the marshes, the excitement of the scores and hundreds of ducks that you would see every afternoon, passing high overhead, even if none came within range, and the sense of an archaic, princely heritage that hung around the avenues of mossy oaks, the old houses, and even the dikes and ditches. You were a long way, psychologically speaking, from the cramped calculations and limiting realities of town.

I describe all this as though it happened often. It did not. Two years after I got well, Mrs. Wilson died, Chicora was sold, and that ended our duck-hunting there. Thereafter, trips to the rice-fields were rare—once a season; twice a season, at most—as guests of somebody's friend or cousin. Perhaps I was fortunate. The country never lost its magic; the stories never grew stale; and I never learned to see through the laughter and conviviality to whatever resentments, distances, and exasperations lay beneath. The life we glimpse can be more potent than the one we live. It seemed that Ricky and I were seeing our fathers and their friends in an incarnation of themselves that was not merely earlier, but also more authentic and essential. I daydreamed so much about one day living in a whitewashed board-and-batten cabin in the ricefields, becoming a guide who would tell stories and show the country to novices like myself, that the dreaming now gets into the remembering, like mud into a well. I imagined living my way backwards into the world their stories came from: the asphalt would crack; you would cross at Yauhannah on a flat-bed ferry; every year there would be more ducks than the year before. The plantation houses and oaks and ricefields would remain as they were, because they had not changed in the first place.

This kind of fantasizing received no authorization, direct or indirect, from Daddy himself. He accepted the world he lived in. He relished the duck-hunting and the companionship, and I believe that his company was always very welcome, that the others would have found the hunting less if he had not been there. But he did not need illusion, or perhaps he understood the dependencies and vulnerabilities that illusion fosters. He knew how to hunt, though— no doubt about that. Once Mr. Harper and I shared a blind at one end of a pond, and Daddy was by himself in a skimpy blind at the other end. Late in the morning, a single pintail came over, saw Daddy's decoys, and got interested. He was wary, and circled the blind again and again, staying well out of range. Crouched in our own blind, we could see the pintail twisting his neck as he circled, trying to get a better view. It went on for a good ten minutes, as though Daddy and the duck were having some sort of contest. Finally the circles began to tighten; the duck was edging into range. Mr. Harper fretted—"Why don't he shoot? That duck's going to shy off, next thing you know. He ain't going to get any closer." Daddy never budged, and when the duck made a wider turn, it looked like Mr. Harper had been right. He made two more wide circles, and then started dropping down, not flying so high. It was sunny; you could see the beautiful head and neck, the soft, gray-barred plumage of the back. Then he took a narrower turn, and came back on a course that would carry him straight over the blind. It was like he was giving up; he *had* to find out if anybody was in the blind. Still Daddy didn't stand. "He must be *asleep* in there," Mr. Harper said. But when the duck was directly overhead, Daddy stood, not hurriedly, and swung the gun. The duck never saw him, never flared. There was the one shot and the bird closed up like a book and fell—a brisk, definitive transaction, concluded with a splash. Mr. Harper stood up in our blind and doffed his hat. "I'll vow," he said. "That Franklin."

But for all that, Daddy could take the ricefields or leave them. He would have been happy to see them close the season on ducks for a decade, to give them a chance to recover their numbers. As long as he had even a half-decent bird dog and a few farms where he could go quail-hunting, maybe just for an hour or two in the afternoon, he was happy. And the fact is that I grew up doing much more quail-hunting than duck-hunting, and was much better at it. But duck-hunting promised a whole life, and I knew men who lived for it and through it more intensely than they lived in any other way. When I go duck-hunting in Maine now, those are the men I take with me. Especially Mr. C. C. Harper.

A few years ago, Daddy wrote to say that Mr. Harper had died. It came as no surprise. He had been sick for a long time. When I would go down for a visit, at Christmas or in the spring, Daddy and I would call on him. Daddy would telephone first, to be sure Mr. Harper felt up to having company. He always did, and would be up, dressed in his pajamas, bathrobe, and slippers, when we arrived. Mrs. Harper would sit talking with the three of us for a while, long enough to be sure that Mr. Harper was comfortable, then she would disappear into the kitchen or upstairs. When she came back, half-hour or forty-five minutes later, that meant it was time for him to lie back down. Daddy would rise and say we had to be going; Mr. Harper would say for us to drop by again. And I could remember back to the fifth grade, when he would come by our house in the unannounced way that people did, and find a pretext for walking back to my room and chatting for a few minutes. One time it was to bring me my Christmas present—a box of .410 shells, #5 shot. The card on it said NEXT YEAR.

Daddy said something else in his letter. He said that Mr. Harper had been the one man he had ever felt free to confide in. That surprised me. Mr. Harper was not what you would have called a successful man—he had worked as a clerk or salesman at various stores and agencies around town—and I now know that drinking had a great deal to do with it, although I had no sense of that as a boy. I took it for granted then that everything around me was all right and would go on that way—dull, for the most part, but not subject to significant mutation, and containing no hidden mysteries of shame or pain. It would not have occurred to me that my father or any of his friends would ever have any need, or any thing, to confide. I was naturally aware of parts of myself that needed to be kept secret, and were embarrassments to me, but I assumed they were like bed-wetting, and that I would grow out of them as I had grown out of it. Of course, Mr. Harper drank; I don't remember my father sustaining a significant friendship with any man who didn't. Mr. Harper was always called C. C., even by his own family, and once somebody jokingly proposed new initials for him: I. W. That caught on for a while, and everybody called him I. W. Harper, which thereupon became his favorite bourbon, if it hadn't been already. Every Christmas, he and Daddy would solemnly present each other with a bottle of it.

Even in his pajamas, with the fragile and shrivelled look of terminal illness on him, you could, without much effort of imagination, flesh him out to the size he had been. He still had the broad face, bushy and comically expressive eyebrows, and the coarse, close-cropped, vigorous hair that he had had in his prime. His laugh was weaker, but you could hear in it the two things that were always there. The first was his good nature, even what people would have spoken of as C. C.'s good-heartedness. The other was more complicated. It was an undertone of puzzlement, the kind of laughter you hear from somebody who feels himself an outsider among insiders, and who loves the company but isn't always sure that he understands the joke. As a boy, I certainly never thought of his laughter this way. It simply sounded natural to me, like my own. He was bigger than Daddy or any of his friends, thickset as a bear and with something of a bear's unlikely quickness and agility, but he was, to a child, less distant and intimidating than other adults. That was all.

He finally had to give up drinking, but that was after I had left Conway, and after drink had pretty well done its work. I suppose he now looked back at all our times of hunting and fishing as he did at the whiskey that had always been a part of them—a bigger part than I knew. He could take no pleasure in those memories and those stories. That would have been a nostalgia for what had ruined him. Instead, he would ask me about Maine, and the hunting there. I described Merrymeeting Bay—a big body of fresh water, but tidal, and with fine marshes. "Sounds like the rice-fields," he said. "Do you have to know somebody to hunt there?" I told him no, it was strictly first come, first served, and he laughed and said that *that* sure didn't sound like the ricefields. And if the hunting was any good, that didn't sound much like them either; from what everybody was telling him, duck-hunting in the rice-fields had just about played out. I made some sort of comment about how we had at least had a few good days down there; I hoped he might relent, and remember some of the pleasure of it. But he didn't. There was just that bleak satisfaction—the hunting had played out; he wouldn't be missing much. As far as remembering it went, I was going to have to do that on my own.

There were the stories that I heard more than once; there were those ranked formations of ducks, passing high overhead, that we would see every afternoon; and the expectancy of the night before, the rising in the dark, the whispered, fervent cordiality when we would gather in somebody's kitchen for a three A.M. breakfast, before the long drive down to the ricefields. The greatest expectation of all was Opening Day, and when I was fifteen, we were all invited down for it—Daddy, Mr. Cox, Mr. Harper, Mr. McIver, Ricky, and I. At least that is the way I remember it, although I know that my memory of those times keeps merging characters and events from one hunt with characters and events from another, trying to make a whole story out of a lot of fractured ones.

We stayed in a cabin—a sort of clubhouse that had been built back in the twenties, after the original house had burned down or been demolished. We had got down late on a Friday afternoon before the season opened on Saturday, and at dusk had walked along a dike in what was always called the House Field—a marsh just adjacent to the landing. It was the time of day when, during the season, you could almost always see the ducks headed out to open water to spend the night. But because nothing had yet disturbed them here, they were dropping into the House Field and the fields across the river in numbers I had never seen before—certainly in hundreds, and probably in thousands. They seemed oblivious to us, although we were talking and in plain sight. There was a hubbub of quacking and all the other noises that ducks make—the almost disembodied whistle of pintails, softer than a widgeon's; the rising, unduck-like squealing of wood ducks. We stayed until it was too dark to see any more, although late comers were still arriving—you could hear the hissing of their wings as they came over. It was turning cold; the weather was driving them to us.

I don't remember what all the considerations were, but it was decided that Mr. Harper and I would hunt together the following morning. I waked up not long after midnight, and went outside to pee. There was a high, bright moon, and it was very frosty. I knew that I would not get back to sleep that night. I walked down to the edge of the House Field and listened. All the ducks that we had seen were silent now; there was just the unearthly moonlit stillness of a winter night. It was a kind of perfect balancing of peace and anticipation, a predator's moment of pastoral assurance.

But it did not go well for me and Mr. Harper. We were to hunt a field that lay across the river and upstream, and on our way to it, we hit something in the dark—a snag or floating log—and broke the shear pin on the motor. We didn't have a spare, and so we had to paddle the rest of the way. We paddled as hard as we could, but shooting had already started by the time we got into the field, and the sun was clearing the tree line before we reached the blind. As we were pulling the boat into the blind, two wood duck came over, and by a long and lucky shot I killed one. It fell on the far side of the pond, so I shoved the boat back out of the blind and paddled across to get it. When I was in the middle of the pond, a flock of big duck—blacks or mallards—showed up, flying low and coming our way. I crouched and kept myself so still it seemed like praying, but I might as well have been trying to hide in the middle of an unoccupied basketball court. The ducks flared and Mr. Harper shot, but they were miles out of range.

After that we sat. It was cold, windy, and bright. There is a magic time in duck-hunting—the half light that precedes the actual rising of the sun, when the cold night air raises a white mist off the water, and the possibility of birds seems to inhere in the low threshold of visibility, as though that were as much their habitat as the marshes themselves. As the visibility increases, you feel the possibilities evaporating in the sunlight, and finally everything is bare and exposed around you. The ducks fly high and can see everything; the decoys seem like a ludicrous expedient; and the adventure ebbs out of the morning.

We stayed a long time; it was nearly noon when we picked up the decoys and started back. I paddled, so Mr. Harper could at least have one more chance of getting a duck. The tide was low, but, even so, I turned us into a side ditch, a dead end that might conceivably have a duck in it. If I had been by myself, I wouldn't have bothered, but when you are paddling somebody else, you want to make a bit of a fuss over them. We got to the end of the ditch; there was nothing. That was that. We pushed the boat backwards down the ditch, using the paddles as poles, until it widened enough for us to turn around, and then we both paddled back to the main ditch. Mr. Harper wanted to keep on paddling—it was cold, and the exercise felt good—-but, to humor me, he picked up his gun, and I paddled us on down the ditch, trying to do it the way Robert would have done it, quick and quiet. But it was cold enough for both of us to be thinking more about the cabin and food than about hunting. He yawned and shivered, stretched his legs out in front of him and crossed his ankles and tried to make himself comfortable.

And that was the story we shared, the one that, twenty years later, I hoped he might remember with pleasure. Of course we went blithely around the last corner in the ditch, and it all happened as fast as a hiccup: that panicky rush of wings that feels like it is inside your shirt; Mr. Harper yanking himself up—Gah-RAY!— the exclamation cut off by the gun. It was a twelve-gauge pump, side ejection. I know it was side ejection because it seemed to me that he shot so fast that the third shell was spinning out of the chamber before the first one had hit the water. And it seemed like the first black duck was arrested in its flight, then the second, then the third, and they all hung in the air for an instant, no longer going up and not yet coming down, and then all fell together. I had never seen shooting like that before—that fast, that sure— and I have never seen it since. It was shocking.

The others were already in by the time we got back to the landing. It was my story to tell, not Mr. Harper's, because I could boast about his shooting. All the men professed not to believe it: "I. W., now you shot them ducks on the water and you know it and you might as well admit it." "Tell the truth and shame the devil, I. W.—who'd you buy 'em off of?" That was affection, the kind of backhanded compliment that they would pay each other. Daddy said drily that anybody who had ever seen I. W. shoot would know that what we had here was a pure and simple case of Involuntary Duckslaughter in a Heat of Passion, and there wasn't much risk of his being a repeat offender. As far as I know, Daddy was right about that—at least I never saw Mr. Harper do any very impressive shooting again. But Daddy told me later, back in Conway, that he had seen C. C. do something like that three or four times before. "When he ain't got time to think about it, your Godfather's still about the best wingshot I ever saw—even better than Mr. Ned Cox. But when he's got the time, he might be about the worst."

I don't remember where we hunted that afternoon, and it doesn't matter. I don't remember what we had for supper, but the preparation of it was always the same. Mr. Harper would run everybody out of the kitchen, and in my memory it is like a cartoon, smoke and clatter coming through the door, and much urgent imprecation—"Come back heah, you sorry scoundrel"—as though he were trying to corner, subdue, and fry something that still had a lot of fight in it. He would finally emerge, smiling, sweating, and triumphant, with the food heaped on platters. Everybody ate; Mr. Cox, a pretty serious trencherman, would take a mouthful and chew it in his attentive and wary way, and say, "Well you surprise me, Collins Crawford Harper. This could be worse," and Mr. McIver would say, "Now Ned, don't challenge him." It would be porkchops and cornbread and mustard greens, or fried fish and hushpuppies and slaw—good solid country fare, and only a little scorched around the edges. After we ate whatever we ate that night, Ricky and I washed up, and when we came back into the big room, they were sitting around the table, playing penny-ante poker.

They hadn't necessarily grown up together, but they had grown up in towns so much alike, and with such a similarity of codes and decorums, that you would have thought they all shared one childhood—even Mr. Cox, who was from Mississippi. Maybe sharing one childhood means nothing more than sharing one set of disguises, and perhaps their stories were just an informal *lingua franca*, an artificial way of establishing a comity. But it never sounded that way to me.

As they played cards that night—itself the occasion for a lot of laughter and, from my standpoint, a fine spectator sport—they somehow got off on the war. All of them had been in it, although most, like Daddy, had been beyond draft age when it came. He had a funny story about that—how, after he had received his orders to report for officer's training, he had taken a last quail-hunting trip out toward Hickory Grove, where Mr. Pig Johnson had a farm. Mr. Pig figured in a good many stories—he was the sort of stiff-necked, litigious countryman who was always getting in a dispute over property lines or stray hogs. He would seek counsel, pay if he could, and urge Daddy to make up the rest by coming out and bird-hunting at his place as often as he pleased. Daddy said the bird-hunting wasn't especially good, but he felt obligated to go out there often enough for Mr. Pig to feel that the account was settled, so that he could, as Daddy put it, "go right on look-ing airy man straight in the eye, unbowed, unbeholden, and unbathed." And that was why he had gone out there late in the winter of 1942, a month or so before I was to be born. He found Mr. Pig out back; they talked about this and that, and Daddy mentioned that he would be going into the service soon. Mr. Pig commiserated—they didn't have no right to go and draft a fambly man like that. Daddy said that actually he hadn't been drafted; he'd volunteered. Mr. Pig looked at him, turned and spat, and said, "Well, hit aint fur me to say and ever man's got to hoe his own roe on his own time. But lawyer, be durnt if I be the kind of hard-hearted man as would go off and leave my wife a widder with a bunch of pore little orphants like that. *Durnt* if I be."

This was a story I heard often, as it was a great favorite of Mama's—she sharing, I believe, some of Mr. Pig's reservations about a superfluous and evitable patriotism. And from the way the men talked about the war, you'd have thought it really had been a kind of lark for them, one more dimension of the common ground they shared. Their houses always had one or two books of pho-tographs—*Life's Picture History of World War II* was a popular one—and maybe a collection of the Bill Mauldin Willy and Joe cartoons, or some exciting, eyewitness account of the Guadalcanal campaign or the Battle of Britain. It was like a college they had all gone to—they cherished its memorabilia and the evidence of their association with it. In our attic Daddy still had his helmet, and cowrie shells that he had picked up on the beaches of Tinian. In cold weather he liked to wear the heavy blue-black wool shirt that had been standard naval issue. Mr. McIver for some reason owned a few cases of C-rations; once he allowed Ricky and me to open a can, and eat the dry, insipid chocolate bars it contained.

Best of all, and contrary to all regulations, Mr. Harper had a German gun. It was not a military weapon but a sporting one, a beautifully made over-and-under: sixteen-gauge shotgun on top; medium-calibre deer rifle on bottom. The stock was walnut; the receiver was finely engraved with a hunting scene of a boar and hounds. He only used the gun for target practice—it wasn't well suited to our kind of hunting—and he had often let me handle it. Breaking the gun open and snapping it shut was like slamming the door on a Rolls Royce. It never occurred to me to wonder how he had come by the gun. Was the German army at the end finally reduced to using such things? Was it loot, booty, or something traded by a civilian in exchange for ration coupons or a warm coat? I suppose I thought of it as having exactly the same status as the athletic trophies he had won back in high school and college, and that were displayed on a shelf in his dining room.

I don't know how Ricky felt about it. I felt that the two of us had missed the boat. There would be no war for us to go adventuring in and tell stories about; even the hunting now was mostly just a way of evoking the stories about how it had been. I could imagine myself becoming far more satisfactory than I was, but I could not imagine that I, or Ricky, or any of our contemporaries would ever become as unself-conscious, vivid, funny, and *happy* as those men were when they did things together, told stories and provided fodder for new stories. Even if it was something that had happened only last year, a story put it into a perspective of comic innocence; you never thought of the humiliations or hard feelings that might have been involved.

So that night they played poker and talked about the war. The bottle was on the table, and when they opened a bottle on these trips, Mr. Harper threw away the cap or cork. When they opened the second bottle, he did the same thing: "We ain't going to take back any cripples." Ricky and I went out onto the back porch, and, under the single dim bulb there, we cleaned the ducks—not a bad job at all, but a slow one, and cold. By the time we came back in, we were pretty tired, and went ahead and unrolled our sleeping bags on the floor, and crawled in. Then we could lie there and listen to the clattering of chips on the table and the talking.

Mr. McIver had a long involved yarn about Lieutenant Boyd Anderson and the Italian war widow—how she thought he was going to marry her, merely because he had promised to ("Boyd was one of the nicest fellas you ever met in your life, and he didn't like to risk hurtin' anybody's feelings about anything by telling 'em the truth if he could possibly avoid it"); how Lieutenant Anderson prevailed on Captain McIver to go and tell the widow that he'd just died a hero's death, that very afternoon. There was something about Mr. McIver standing on the door stoop breaking this tragic news to the widow, and her all weeping and distraught ("I felt so bad about it I almost told her the truth, but then I figured *that* wouldn't cheer her up much either"), and about that time this hairy-lookin' fella with a towel wrapped around his middle and a carbine in his hand comes busting into the hall behind her, yelling something at Mr. McIver or at the widow—he wasn't sure, and he wasn't sure whether the language was Italian, German, or Brooklyn, and he didn't hang around to find out.

"But Boyd must have made a real impression on her," he said, and went on to say how after the war was over, every year for a good many years the war widow would send over a letter with some lire in it, explaining how dear Boyd had been her fiancé, and had told her all about the wonderful town he lived in—Florence, South Carolina, just like Florence, Italy—and how on this, the anniversary of his death, she wished to have flowers placed in church for him, to represent the prayers that she would be offering for his soul. The letter would be addressed simply to Florist, Florence, S.C., U.S.A. And Mr. McIver told how the postman would always deliver it to the same flower shop, because he had a cousin there who needed the business. And how the florist would grimly go down to the bank and, with great difficulty, get the lire rendered into dollars and cents, and then go back to the shop, make up the tackiest bouquet that that amount of money could buy, wrap green tissue paper around it, and take it home and stonily present it to her husband of nearly twenty years, Mr. Boyd Anderson. I lay on the floor listening to him tell that story and watching the firelight play on the ceiling, and ached with trying not to laugh.

Because it was Saturday night, we wouldn't be hunting the next morning, and nobody seemed inclined to go to bed. The men had begun recalling all sorts of things from the war—all those gritty details about food, about life on a troop ship, about trying to sleep, about all the strange people, from every walk of life and every section of the country, that they were thrown with. I was sleepy and interested both. Things were beginning to get blurry, and that finally seemed to be what they were talking about as the night ran down—about how unbelievably confused and chaotic it had all been. When Tinian was buzzing with rumors and mysterious civilians were flying in and out, Daddy was suddenly dispatched with a sealed invoice to Guam. He hitched a ride on a B-17, presented the invoice, and received a light, bulky crate, marked SECRET, flew back to Tinian, and presented the crate to his Captain. Some weeks later, at about the time that the *Enola Gay* was being readied for Hiroshima, he chanced to learn what his secret cargo had been. Three dozen tennis rackets. Unstrung.

Billy Watson's Croker Sack

Mr. Harper said yes, it sure had been that way. He seemed to be saying that it was a wonder that the soldiers had ever got organized enough to find each other and fight, seemed to be talking about the last winter of the war, when the German armies were collapsing and the Allies were advancing and not finding anything in front of them. It was all snow and mud and lost supplies, having things, like Daddy's tennis rackets, that you didn't need, and not having things, like rations or fuel or ammunition, that you did need. I think he was in the engineers, not in a combat unit at all, but with the front breaking up and flowing away, leaving pockets of resistance behind and troopless vacuums ahead, it was hard to tell whether you were within enemy lines or your own. And half the Germans you came upon were only looking for Americans to surrender to: "A lot of them no older than those two jokers sacked out on the floor over there, and looking just about as lively." I didn't know whether Ricky was asleep yet or not. It had been such a day, starting in the dark, a good twenty-four hours ago, when I had gone outdoors to pee, then our breaking the shear pin and all the bright air and open spaces, the cypress-lined creeks and close ditches of the ricefields still in my head, and that instant when the frame froze, and those three black duck were all dead at once in midair. Then supper, plucking the ducks, the laughing, and now trying to stay awake for this one last story.

He had been sent to pick up something or deliver something or relay some message. His jeep had got mired and he had to hitch a ride, or maybe he had fallen in with a motorized convoy that was trying to connect up with the unit he was looking for. It sounded like the first day in a new school, all contradictory instructions and following other people around and nobody knowing who was supposed to be where; but it was a war: the rumbling and thumping of bombing or shelling ahead or off on one flank, the gutted towns, somebody lying dead beside the road. Somebody else shaking him awake, telling him to get his rifle and fall in, and be quiet about it. Four or five of them, no more, moving through the dark, coming up to a place where somebody whispered them to a stop, said lie down: don't talk, don't smoke, don't show a light.

When night lifted it was foggy and hard to see, but it gradually became clear that they were on one side of a narrow, steep ravine. On the other side they could only see woods, nothing else. But directly in front of them were two logs, spiked to trees that grew up from the bottom of the ravine. It took him a minute to figure out that it was a communal privy. "You had to admire 'em. The logs were out over the ravine. The top one was to sit on. The bottom log was like a catwalk, and a gangplank ran out to it from the bank. The logs were about twenty foot long. They'd stripped the bark off both of 'em, and hewed the top flat, like a puncheon floor."

He didn't need to be told, or to tell us, why they were there. But you can't leave a story hanging. They couldn't see anybody on the opposite side, but soon they heard stirring. A motor started up; a man coughed. One soldier appeared out of the woods, walked across the gangplank, and edged his way along the lower log, using the top one as a handrail. He went all the way to the end before pulling down his trousers and seating himself on the top log, his back to them. "That must have been the rule. You had to go to the end of the log—just like at a communion rail—so the next fella to come along wouldn't have to work his way around you. That made sense. They were smart people—smarter than us, I believe. Better organized, anyway. Just not enough of 'em."

They let that first one go. They were starting to smell cooking, and Mr. Harper said how good it smelled, the way all food, no matter how sorry, smells when you are outside in cold weather. I don't know about Daddy and Mr. McIver and Mr. Cox; I don't know whether they had heard this story before, whether it was a special story that Mr. Harper had suddenly decided to tell, or whether it was just another war story. If there was any change in the atmosphere of the room, any turn toward seriousness or suspense, I am not a witness to it. After breakfast the soldiers came filing out of the woods. The log filled up like a hen-roost. The man next to Mr. Harper held up his hand and shook his head: not yet. They let a few more Germans come out of the woods to the edge of the ravine, where they stood and waited their turn. The first man on the log finished, and headed back across the gang-plank. That was when they opened fire, starting with the men on the bank, going on to the ones on the log. One man on the log leaped for a tree in front of him, tried to get the trunk between himself and the shooting, the way a squirrel would.

"Then we got out of there," said Mr. Harper. "Lickety-split and hell for election. And you know when we got back far enough to feel safe, we just fell on the ground. I mean we all fell right down *on the ground*, we were laughing so hard. I tell you it seemed like the funniest thing in the world at the time. And I'll tell you some-thing else, too. I don't believe I took a crap, properly speaking, from then to V-E Day, and that's the truth. Man, I was sho' glad to see that war end."

Somebody else remembered something else. Mr. Harper's story became like a bizarre sequence of cards that had been dealt during an evening of penny-ante—something you might remember briefly, but something that would mostly get shuffled under, reabsorbed back into the deck. You played the hand you were dealt, and exclaimed or laughed about it afterwards. Maybe you liked to gamble, liked the thrill and the bluff and risk of it. Well you could do it, but the stakes were going to remain small. Nobody was going to let you win enough or lose enough to jeopardize the game, to embarrass or dampen or discompose the company. That was the way they did it, as far as I was ever able to see—the way they played cards, told stories, hunted ducks, carried on their friendship. Yet somewhere along the line, Daddy and Mr. Harper confided in each other. I guess Daddy's even asking him to be my godfather, back there in the early days of the war, with both of them soon to be shipping out, was a kind of confiding in itself.

And apparently it continued through all that followed, not affected by one man's fortune and the other man's misfortune, or by one man's inability to handle the bottle they exchanged every Christmas.

I don't know whether these things hold together and make sense. They are present to me through hunting. You can lose your nerve, talking about someone who didn't talk much, and trying to understand or explain him. He lived what he was, and is out of range of the questions which I would, in any case, have hardly known how to put to him. He always remembered my birthday, and even after I was a grown man with children I would get a card every year. No message on it—just the printed birthday greetings and his name: "Mr. Harper." He always signed it like that, put quotation marks around it, as though it were a small joke between us.

It might have been the Sunday that had already arrived by the time Ricky and I finally got to sleep, or it might have been the following Sunday or the one after that. We were in church. As was often the case, we were without a preacher, the congregation being too small to attract a full-time resident clergyman very often, or keep him very long. It was Daddy's turn to be lay-reader; he, Mr. Harper, and Mr. D. W. Green shared that job in an informal rotation. They could not preach or administer sacraments, but they could lead the congregation through the Order for Morning Prayer, read the appointed Lesson and Epistle, and choose, in consultation with the organist, the hymns for the day. I knew the words to the service long before I considered their meaning. The prayers, thanksgivings, and supplications were all a sort of droning hum we made together, generally indicative of resignation and respect. I much preferred this to the laborious, personal, uplifting discussions that we were supposed to have in Sunday school.

We were in the second hymn. It was familiar; they all were familiar, because the organist's repertoire was small. Mr. and Mrs.

Harper were in their usual pew, directly across from Mama and me. He wore glasses—wire-rimmed bifocals—for church, and of course he wore a suit. He was one of those people who surprise you when they put on formal clothes. They wear them exactly as they would wear any other clothes, and so they look comfortable, as though they had been born to dress that way. The glasses were another matter. He still had to hold the prayer book or hymnal far out from him, and study it with a sort of humorous exasperation, squinting and drawing a bead on it. He looked like Smoky the Bear trying to impersonate Erasmus.

Most of us sang in the same close-mouthed way—an earnest, amplified whisper, as close to tuneless as you could get and still call it singing. Even Mr. Harper, with his big voice, did it like that. So I was mumbling along with the rest, running my eyes ahead of the verse we were singing, down to the last verse, and reading it in the same idle way you might read a leaflet lying on the bench beside you in a bus station. Then I read it again and then we were singing it. I looked up at Daddy; he was singing absently while he opened the book to the Epistle for the day. I looked at Mr. Harper. His face was serious and thoughtless, the way your face is supposed to be in church. He was singing with everybody else, so I sang too, if you could call it that:

> Time LIKE an EV-er FLOW-ing STREAM
> Bears ALL her SONS a-WAY;
> They DIE for-GOT-ten AS the DREAM
> Dies AT the OPE-ning DAY.

And then we were in the middle of the long, drawn out Ahhhh-MEN, and he was closing the hymnal and we were all sitting down for the Epistle. As he sits, his face comes up for an instant, looking into mine. He grins at me and winks, quick as the clicking of a shutter.

Billy Watson's Croker Sack

When I had finished writing the first of these essays, "A Snapping Turtle in June," I sent it to Deanne Urmy, to get her reaction. She wrote back with some suggestions that proved very valuable, and also with a question. What was a "croker sack"? Did I mean a cracker sack, and if so, what was that?

It is always dangerous to question college professors. They are paid to talk by the hour.

Dear Deanne,

I was surprised that you didn't know what a croker sack was, and further surprised to find that *Webster's New World Dictionary*, *Webster's Third International Dictionary*, and the *Oxford American Dictionary* didn't know either. I had to go to several dictionaries of Americanisms to find it, and even then the results weren't profoundly satisfactory.

In South Carolina the word referred to any biggish cloth sack—

for example, the hundred-pound sacks that livestock feed came in. It was a word like any other; I'm certain that nobody thought of it as quaint or archaic. If there was anything notable about it, it was that country people were likely to mispronounce it—*croakus sack*—and we town folk found this an amusing rustic illiteracy. I didn't know where the word originated, but then we seldom know the origins of the words we so blithely bandy about. There was one plausible etymology right at hand, no farther away than Mishoe's Fish Market: a *croaker* is a small, abundant fish of the drum family, which can be caught in any tidal inlet. For all I know, they might have been caught by the sackful, and from what I know of their taste, it is easy to imagine two men dividing up the day's catch, and one saying to the other: "Look, you take the croakers and I'll take the *croaker sack*." Folk etymology is a minor form of myth-making; it gives plausible explanations about how things came to be as they are.

Real etymology, however, is a minor form of science, and, like science, it requires much more credulity than the myths it supplants. We have to abandon the evidence of our senses and the logic of our experience, and trust entirely to methods that maintain their authority by reducing everything else to absurdity. No myths about the origins of life or the nativity of the stars are as staggeringly implausible as the accounts of these events we receive from biologists and astrophysicists. *Credo quia absurdum est* is a first principle of science as well as of theology. And, I might add, with much recent evidence to support me, of literary exegesis as well, but perhaps this digression has digressed far enough.

To return to *croker sack*. It has nothing to do with croakers. There is absolutely no historical evidence to support it. *To croak*, of course, is also *to die*, and this inelegant colloquialism has been around for a surprisingly long time. So maybe a croker sack was a body bag? This conjecture (like the one about the fish) has in fact been conjectured, but it too has no historical evidence.

Nor was a croker sack used in the collecting of frogs.

Postscript: Billy Watson's Croker Sack

In the fourteenth century, Englishmen, on crusade in the Holy Land, discovered saffron, which was widely used as a dye and a medicine, and only incidentally as a spice. They thought enough of it to smuggle some bulbs back to England with them, on the unlikely chance that a spiky, bright-blossomed little plant which thrived in the arid heat of the eastern Mediterranean would flourish in the damp and chill of their native land. Implausibility being what it is, the plant in fact flourished to admiration, and soon vast fields of it were established in the dampest and chilliest of all the English shires, Essex and Cambridge. Acres of them were grown in the reclaimed bogs and fens; it must have looked like the tulip fields of Holland. By the sixteenth century, the little town of Walden, in Essex, had acquired its present name of Saffron Walden. But in the latter eighteenth century, a mysterious fungus showed up, and it, combined with the development of new and cheaper dyes, ended commercial saffron production in England.

Saffron is collected from the pistils of the autumnal crocus, which looks exactly like the familiar springtime crocus except that it is always blue, never white or red or yellow. Saffron was sometimes called *crocus*, and a saffron dealer was called a croker.

Aha. One pounces. The dealer had a sack and that was called a croker's sack until the second *s* swallowed the first and it became a croker sack. Nope. The *Oxford English Dictionary*, all twelve volumes of it, plus supplements, records nothing for *croker* (or *croccer* or *croaker* or *crocus*) sack, bag, etc. Croker sacks are purely American. And highly regional. They are most likely to be encountered in coastal Georgia, coastal South Carolina, piedmont Virginia, and Martha's Vineyard. They are occasionally met with elsewhere, presumably as transplants, but they don't really flourish except in the places I have mentioned. There are people who study these things as meticulously as ornithologists study, let us say, the migration route and breeding grounds of the Kirtland's warbler, of which more later. These highly specialized folk (it's a tough way to make a living, but nobody's gotta do it) have also determined that the illiterate rustic form—*croakus sack*—was in fact the "correct" or at least the original one. *Croker* came into being when the *s* of *sack* swallowed the *s* of *crocus*, leaving *crok-uh*, which then succumbed to what is known as the retroflexive final *r* (I think this is the same thing you hear in the way that many people, including the entire population of Massachusetts, pronounce *parka: parker*). Both the evidence of research and the laws of linguistic mutation leave no doubt about this: *crocus* readily degenerates into *croker; croker* does not degenerate into *crocus*. We town folk were the ones who had it wrong.

Well then: saffron must have been a big item of the transatlantic trade. Maybe they ate tons of it on their rice in Georgia and South Carolina; it was no doubt shipped in sacks on vessels captained and crewed by old salts from Martha's Vineyard. Nothing could be simpler. Some saffron, or at least some of the sacks it came in, found its way to piedmont Virginia. Or maybe it went the other way. Maybe after the great crocus blight ruined England, they grew crocuses in the southeast and exported saffron, via ships out of Martha's Vineyard, to England, or India, or the Canary Islands, or Davey Jones's locker.

But of course we know the fatuity of that speculation, because we know what saffron is. It is the most expensive spice in the world. A pound of it requires that 75,000 crocus blossoms be painstakingly plucked, dried, and scraped. Cocaine is cheap as fatback by comparison There seem to have been few times in recorded history when an ounce of saffron was worth less than an ounce of gold. One croker sack full would suffice to feed an entire county all the saffron it could stand for approximately 350 years, assuming that the cost of it had left the people in the county money enough to buy any food to sprinkle it on. And there is no history of commercial saffron production in the south Atlantic states.

That is about where the story ends. Conjecture's last gasp is this: saffron, being so hideously expensive, might have been packed

in little sacks of special weave, so that not one precious grain of
it could leak out. Cloth so woven might become known as crocus
cloth. In defence of this, we may observe that cloths have a funny
way of getting their start and their names in one place, and then
achieving their real identity centuries later, in a world inconceiv-
able to the original weavers. In the seventeenth century, the little
manufacturing town of Nîmes, in southern France, produced a
fine, tough cloth that became known and esteemed as *serge de Nîmes*.
To the southeast, Genoa had long since given its name to a tough
cotton twill. In the course of time, vowels eroded, syllables elided
or vanished; words approximated the mutations of human or natural history. You probably know where this takes us. It takes us
to the mythic American west, as manufactured and merchandised
from Hong Kong to Freeport, Maine. One should consider that
while putting on one's *jeans*, which are, of course, made from *denim*.
So, perhaps, with crocus or croker cloth. It had no more logical
or direct connection to the south Atlantic states and Martha's
Vineyard than Genoa or Nîmes did to Dodge City, or Abilene,
or Tombstone, Arizona, or Calvin Klein, but somehow it caught
on and thrived there, as implausibly as those bright crocuses from
the Holy Land in the fields of Essex.

There is early evidence to support the notion that *crocus* at one
time referred to a material, and not a sack. In 1687, Joseph Proutt,
leading a military expedition in the vicinity of what is now Proutt's
Neck, Maine, wrote to the Governor and Council of Massachusetts. He was in desperate need of resupply—powder, shot, and
shoes were all used up or worn out. There were no beds or blankets for the wounded: "here is great want of beds, or *crocus* to
make straw beds." Nine years later, we find a book with the arrest-
ing title of *God's Protecting Providence ... evidenced in the Remarkable
Deliverance of Divers Persons from the Devouring Waves of the Sea, amongs
which they Suffered Shipwrack; and also from the more cruelly Devouring Jaws
of the Cannibals of Florida*, by a Quaker named Jonathan Dickinson,
who had undertaken to ship himself and his family from Port Royal,

Jamaica, to Philadelphia, Pennsylvania. As the title implies, the trip was not uneventful. After being shipwrecked, Dickinson, his wife, infant son, and a good many others were taken captive by Indians, who stripped them all naked and exposed them to many indignities, not the least of which were mosquitoes and sand-gnats. Eventually, their captors seem to have grown tired of tormenting them, and took them to an Indian village somewhere south of St. Augustine and began to treat them with some decency: "The old Casseekey [chief or king] fetched some water, and washed Robert Barrow's feet, and my wife's; after which he got some *canvas and crocus ginger bags*, which they had got out of a vessel that was cast on shore. . . . My wife had two pieces of sail canvas given her, and I with the others had each a crocus ginger bag." Ginger, we learn elsewhere in the narrative, was part of the cargo, so *crocus* here must refer to the material of which the bags were made.

There is still a problem. The sack given to Dickinson was obviously big—he was able to fashion some sort of garment from it—and Proutt's letter pretty clearly implies that *crocus* was coarse stuff, not the tightly woven sort of thing you'd expect saffron to be packed in. All citations of the material, including my own, indicate that it is something like burlap. Maybe it was used to carry crocus bulbs in, although it seems remarkable that a special cloth would have evolved for so elementary a function.

Kirtland's warbler nests in a very small territory—roughly sixty by one hundred miles—in north central Michigan, close along the banks of the celebrated (by trout fishermen) Ausable River. And it nests there only in groves of young jackpines. If the trees are taller than eighteen feet, the warbler shuns them. Jackpines themselves are a curiosity. Throughout their range, they are pyrophiles, fire-lovers, germinating in the aftermath of a forest fire, establishing themselves in thick groves, growing, producing their seeds, and dying. The seeds patiently wait until God's Protecting

Providence sends the fire next time. So the Kirtland's warbler is a sort of delayed Phoenix; it rises out of the ashes, or at least out of the trees that rise out of the ashes. It is only slightly less rare than the Phoenix; there are about a thousand or fifteen hundred of them, nesting in the pine groves around Mio, Michigan (where the jackpines are now artificially kept at the optimum level), wintering in the Bahamas, and very rarely seen anywhere in between.

Once there was no doubt a logic to it, some reason why this otherwise rather ordinary-appearing warbler evolved itself into such ecologically reduced circumstances. But that logic lies buried in a history older than logic itself, probably having to do with glaciation, the heavings and subsidings of the earth, the spreading and disappearing of certain ecosystems, changes of climate, and other such greater and lesser transformations of the planet. Someday, the Kirtland's inexplicably rigid proclivities may help illustrate some bold new thesis about one chapter of the earth's unwitnessed history; someday, too, croker sacks may explain things about more recent, but still obscure, patterns of migration, settlement, and connectedness.

In the meantime, nobody doubts that the warbler ought to be preserved. The town of Mio has erected a large statue to it, and ornithologists flock to the jackpine groves every spring—a migration at least as strange, if you think about it, as the one that it intends to study. You cannot erect a statue to a word, and the odds do not favor the survival of a word whose currency has shrunken to so small a territory. About all you can do is use it, and perhaps one reader in a thousand will track it down, and begin to speculate on its odd history, and move from there into speculations that we cannot predict.

It pleases me how both the bird and the word have managed to outlast the circumstances that formed them. We think of nature and history both as belonging to the opportunists, the ones who teach us how to adapt, evolve, seize the day, or fill the niche. On the whole, we are right to think this way, but the world is also full of quirky and implausible survivors, things that still live, as neurotic people do, by a logic that eludes or defies us, because it is rooted somewhere out of sight. Their abnormality, their peculiarity, is the small aperture through which our normality gets a peek at the deeper structure of things, and learns to see beyond its own conventions and assumptions.

I guess I also have a more personal and self-concerning reason for wanting to keep the word as it is, instead of supplying some perfectly appropriate and familiar substitute, like *burlap bag* or *gunny sack*. It is one of those things that I feel too strongly to express clearly. It has to do with my relation to the community I lived in, the people I knew, and the things I saw, handled, heard, and spoke about every day. I assumed that it was all commonplace, universal, and without distinction or interest of any sort. Now, as I begin to write about it, I more and more conclude that what is undistinguished can nevertheless turn out to be genuinely and stubbornly distinctive. I very much fear that writing about such a place will come out sounding like "local color." The writer who consciously defines himself as a local colorist has two options, both bad. He can take the vantage point of the outside world, assume a tone of cosmopolitan urbanity, and portray a quaint, picturesque, amusingly or endearingly or appallingly backward sort of place. This is a patronizing of the subject. Or he may speak as an insider, a native, advertising and merchandising his own assiduously cultivated, artificially preserved provinciality as a way of laying claim to some sort of authenticity. That is a patronizing of the self.

I'm sure my writing won't consistently escape these evasions of the complexities of the particular place, or of the self that looks at it. But the croker sack has quite unexpectedly turned out to be an emblem of what I would hope to find and how I would hope to find it. Your questioning the word made me look at something that had been too familiar for me to see. Once opened for inspection, Billy's sack, squirming with the results of *his* researches, began to reveal more than either of us would ever have expected, imagined, or asked for. It seems in that way like a certain kind of small, inherently insignificant event: a *cul de sac*, but not because it contains nothing and leads nowhere. Rather because it quietly sits there, not exactly inviting inquiry, but refusing to be reduced by explanation, filed away, forgotten.

And that, I'm sure you will agree, is enough on that subject. Everybody here sends greetings to everybody there.

Frank